# PULSE COOKERY

Here is a complete range of recipes using beans, peas and lentils to prepare an astonishing variety of colourful, nutritious and inexpensive pulse dishes.

# PULSE COOKERY

### Wholesome Recipes with Peas, Beans and Lentils

### includes Sweet Dishes

*by*

## PAMELA DIXON

Illustrated by Clive Birch

## THORSONS PUBLISHERS LIMITED
Wellingborough, Northamptonshire

First published 1980

British Library Cataloguing in Publication Data

Dixon, Pamela
   Pulse cookery.
   1. Cookery (Legumes)
   I. Title
   641.6'5'65       TX803.L/

   ISBN 0-7225-0647-3
   ISBN 0-7225-0621-X Pbk

Photoset by Specialised Offset Services Ltd, Liverpool
and printed and bound in Great Britain by
Weatherby Woolnough, Wellingborough
Northamptonshire

# CONTENTS

## Liquid Measure Equivalents

| *British* | *American* |
|---|---|
| 1 teaspoonful | 1¼ teaspoonsful |
| 1 tablespoonful | 1¼ tablespoonsful |
| 1 pint (20 fl oz) | 1¼ pints |

## Cup Measures

A British standard measuring cupful
    contains 10 fl oz (275ml).

An American standard measuring cupful
    contains 8 fl oz (225ml).

# INTRODUCTION

For most of us, bean cookery conjures up a half-forgotten picture of pans simmering on top of the stove for hours – lengthy, leisurely cooking, in fact, from the days when mothers were at home all the time and when fuel was cheap. A new generation of cooks tended to turn away from such methods – they wanted foods which could be quickly prepared, to fit in with working hours and an altogether more hurried lifestyle. But now most of the cheap food has come to an end, and the cheap fuel as well. We are turning back to the natural, nutritious ingredients which have been staple foods down the centuries among the poorer people of the world. But how about that lengthy cooking?

A questioning attitude is a useful attribute in this life, and it applies as much to cooking as to anything else! I have found that, by using a combination of short cuts and modern gadgetry, pulses can be made to cook as fast as potatoes – or faster. I have also found that they can go into *any* course of a meal with complete success – even the pudding.

Pulse recipes are endless, and the ones I have given are necessarily only examples of the many ways in which these wonderfully versatile foods may be used. You will find my versions of some old favourites and also some more unusual ideas, particularly the use of beans as an ingredient in sweet dishes and in rapidly cooked main courses suited to a busy life.

Every time we cook pulses, we are borrowing from hundreds of years of history, for they have been grown and used since records began, from the soya beans of the orient to the lentils used in Egypt and the red beans of South America. There are so many varieties available now that handsome jars of peas, beans and lentils deserve a place in every kitchen. I hope that, as well as enjoying these recipes, you will take them as a basis for experiment and find even more ways of using pulses to help both your menus and your budget.

# What are Pulses?

The name 'pulses' refers to the edible seeds of leguminous plants. The seeds are carried in a pod, large in the case of the bigger beans, right down to small pods on short plants, such as lentils. While some are very distinctive – it is no use, for instance, treating the soya bean in the same way as any of the others – there are many pulses which cook in a similar way and which are virtually interchangeable in recipes.

### Kidney Beans

In this rough classification I would list together black beans, black eyed beans, borlotti (also known as rose cocoa), pinto and red kidney beans. A thoroughly useful and good tempered family, excellent in soups, salads, main dishes and casseroles. They have an agreeable texture, and since they cook reasonably quickly and the skins are not too tough, they are among the best beans to use whole. Be careful if pressure cooking, as some of them are easily turned to a mush if the time given is too long.

### Butter Beans, Haricot Beans, Cannellini and Flageolets

These are also kidney type beans, but the first three are used when white beans are required. Butter beans are large and, when correctly cooked, are nice and mealy, giving plenty of 'substance' to salads and hot dishes. Once again, do not overcook them. Haricots and cannellini are smaller white beans, and any of these three are useful for *pâtés* or spreads which need to be kept a good colour. Flageolets are young haricot beans, remarkably chiefly for their pale green colour. Some of this disappears, of course, when they are cooked, but flageolets do look attractive in a mixture of beans or in salads. Lima beans are rather like butter beans, but are not often obtainable in the U.K.

### Broad Beans and Field Beans

The term 'field beans' covers several varieties of bean including tic and daffa beans, which grow readily in the U.K. Dried broad beans are usually imported and are sometimes hard to find. Broad beans are tasty, but the skins are somewhat tough. Field beans often share this characteristic. They are best in dishes where they can be made into a sieved *purée*, or in soups which will be sieved. Another way of overcoming the problem is dry grinding (see p.19).

## Mung Beans
These little round green beans make the best bean sprouts (see p.24), but they may also be cooked whole for all savoury dishes.

## Adzuki beans
These are little round beans, reddish brown in colour, which are much used in the East. Because they have a sweetish flavour, they are often incorporated into sweetmeats or cooked in dishes with rice. They are fairly easy to find in health food stores, but in most dishes the larger red beans may be satisfactorily substituted.

## Chick Peas
Chick peas are also known by their Spanish name of *garbanzos*. Their use is widespread and recipes come from the mediterranean and the Middle East, and also from India and Mexico. They need either to be soaked well before cooking, or to be prepared by a quick method (see p.20). Their flavour is nutty and distinctive and I find that they may be used like chestnuts in some dishes.

## Soya Beans
A staple food in the East, soya beans have the highest protein content among the pulses. Cooking time varies according to age and type, but soya beans are the most difficult to cook by conventional methods and will always retain a slight 'bite'. Pressure cooking is by far the best way of dealing with them, after which they may be readily incorporated into other dishes. Their very hardness makes them ideal for dry grinding and they are particularly good when ground and toasted (see p.21).

## Split Lentils
You can buy split lentils in a variety of colours, green, yellow, brown and the familiar orange-red. There is usually a good selection in Asian food shops. Split lentils cook fairly quickly and do not need soaking, although this does, of course, shorten the cooking time still further. They break up as they

foods and they have a high fibre content – now recognized to be of considerable importance for our health. They also contain iron, calcium, phosphorus and some of the main vitamins of the B group. An interesting bonus is that when pulses are sprouted (see p.24) their vitamin content is tremendously increased. Sprouted beans are particularly rich in vitamins A and C.

## Cooking Peas, Beans and Lentils

The simplest way of cooking pulses is by the time-honoured method of soaking them overnight and then simmering them in a covered pan until soft. This no doubt began simply as a matter of convenience, part of the rhythm of the household, and indeed if you are going to be at home, it is relatively trouble free. But if this does not suit your way of life it is possible to find lots of short cuts. All that long soaking, for instance, can be replaced in most cases by a shorter soaking time, starting off with hot water. As a guide, the harder the bean, the more it will benefit from soaking. Soya beans, hard as bullets, and also chick peas, respond to long soaking by cooking faster, but there are other ways of dealing with them when time is short, as we shall see.

The middle range of beans – red kidney, black eye, borlotti, etc. – do very well with an hour or so of soaking in hot water, and this may be cut down even more if you are going to pressure cook them. Lentils and split peas need not be soaked at all.

One advantage of copious rinsing and soaking is that it makes pulses more digestible, particularly for those who find that beans and peas produce flatulence. The most important point here, however, is *not* to cook them in the water used for soaking. Another tip for successful cooking is to leave out the salt, which can toughen beans and their skins. I sometimes add salt when putting partly cooked beans into a casserole, but in most dishes I add it at the end. The amount of salt needed may then be gauged more accurately.

*Long Soaking*
Rinse beans in a colander under running cold water, picking them over and removing any damaged beans and grit. Tiny stones often creep into packets of pulses. Soak them for at least

six hours, or overnight, in plenty of cold water to allow room
for the beans to swell. Drain, rinse and drain again. Cook in
water to cover in a heavy pan, or pressure cook them.

*Short Soaking*
Rinse and pick over beans, put them in a large bowl and cover
with boiling water. Leave for one hour, or longer if possible.
Drain, rinse and cook as before.

*Super-quick Method for Pressure Cooking*
Rinse and pick over beans, cover with boiling water and leave
for ten minutes. Drain, rinse and cook. If you have time to
spare while preparing other ingredients to cook with the
beans, drain after ten minutes and repeat the process. This
method is suitable for beans such as red kidney, borlotti, black
eye, etc., which are not among the hardest of the pulses. They
will cook in this way in about 30 minutes.

# Timing

Giving a cooking time for any type of pea, bean, etc., can be
very misleading. It will vary from batch to batch, it will vary
according to the country of origin, and most of all it will vary
according to the age of the bean. Beans from a new season's
crop may cook much faster than those which have been sitting
in the kitchen cupboard for many months. If you have bought
several pounds of one type of bean, it pays to cook a small
amount first and to inspect frequently while cooking. Then
make a note of the result.

The times given on p.13 are, therefore, to be regarded only
as a rough guide. When trying out a different type or batch it
is best to allow plenty of time, for families can be very
unfriendly if they are given hard beans to chew, or worse still,
kept waiting for half an hour while the beans finish cooking!

*Pressure Cooking*
As a general guide, cooking times may be cut by about half
to two-thirds when using a pressure cooker, although, since
timing is more critical, it is even more important to try out a
small amount from a batch of pulses and to note the results.

*Table Showing Conventional Cooking Times for Pulses*

| Type | Cooking Time | Comment |
|------|-------------|---------|
| Kidney beans | 1-1½ hours | Butter beans take longer than smaller beans. Haricot beans are sometimes rather hard. |
| Chick peas | up to 1½ hours | |
| Soya beans | 4 hours | Often impractical, unless you have an Aga type cooker which is always hot. Pressure cooking is more suitable. |
| Adzuki and mung beans | 30-45 mins | |
| Field beans | 45 mins | |
| Broad beans | 1½ hours | |
| Split lentils, soaked unsoaked | 20 mins 45 mins | |
| Continental lentils, soaked unsoaked | 45 mins 1½ hours | |
| Dried peas | 1 hour | |
| Split peas, soaked unsoaked | 30 mins 1 hour | |

For instance, it is very easy to reduce red kidney beans to a mush! The cooking of soya beans is very considerably speeded up – if you intend to finish cooking them with other ingredients, say in a casserole, it is usually possible to soften them adequately in about 30 to 40 minutes.

Lentils and split peas are inclined to froth when pressure

cooked and can clog the valve in the lid. Make sure that recipes including these pulses contain some fat or oil, and if pressure cooking them on their own, put a little cooking oil – two tablespoonsful is usually enough – in the water when you close the cooker.

# Making the Most of Kitchen Gadgets

We have to put up with the dark side of progress, so why not make use of the benefits when we can? Pulses may be cooked in the simplest of cooking pots, but modern gadgets do help if you have to lead a modern life – by which I mean that you suffer from a chronic lack of time, combined with the wish to make food as interesting and delicious as possible. Carefully chosen gadgets do help to cheat the clock, but it is essential to pick the ones which are really going to earn their keep and not sit on the shelf gathering dust.

*Liquidizer*
First class for soup making and for turning cooked pulses into moist *purées*. Less successful sometimes for stiff spreads and *pâtés* as you can spend a lot of time and energy scraping down and removing bits from the blades. Reasonably good for dry grinding, but not to be compared with the purpose-built grinder. A misconception about the liquidizer is that it reduces *everything* to a pulp, even pips. Not so – if you have stringy bits, pips and tough skins in a soup or *purée* they have to be removed by sieving. For a vegetable *purée* made from cooked beans or peas, put them in the goblet with just enough cooking liquid to make the machine run smoothly. Rub the resulting *purée* through a coarse sieve, then reheat it gently with a good knob of butter and seasoning to taste.

*Grinder*
This is the smallest and cheapest bit of electrical help in the kitchen, and is intended chiefly for coffee beans, breadcrumbs, etc. It will grind anything firm and *dry*, and is particularly useful for reducing dry pulses evenly to a fine powder which will cook quickly. Make sure that the base where the powder forms is nice and deep, as some grinders have suffered 'redesigning' lately.

*Food Mill or Salad Maker*

Many electric mixers and mincers have a salad maker attachment, in effect a food mill with interchangeable drums for fine and coarse milling (such as the Moulinex 'Jeanette').

Cooked or partly cooked beans may be put through the machine in the same way as nuts – the one I use turns the beans to an even, mealy texture much faster than I could mash them, and also rejects the coarser skins, which remain in the feed-in channel. The mill is particularly useful for toasted chick-peas (see p.20) or for milling cooked beans for *pâtés* and spreads or cakes. Since it is a relatively dry operation, using it is much less messy than scraping pastes off the blades and goblet of the liquidizer.

*Multi-grater*

The action of the electric food mill is duplicated by the little hand-turned version, also made with interchangeable drums (for example the *Mouli-Master* made by Moulinex). Great for small quantities of firm, cooked beans but fiddly to use for large quantities.

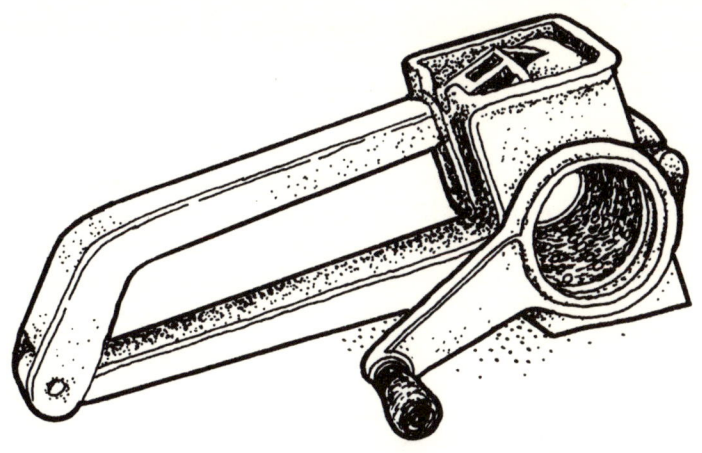

*Mouli-sieve*
The daddy of all kitchen gadgets, and one which stands the test of time, is the Moulinex *Legume*. It is still the best manual aid for mashing cooked potatoes, vegetables or soft, freshly cooked beans.

*Pressure Cooker*

I would not go along with claims that *all* foods taste good when cooked under pressure, but it does make a tremendous difference to the time needed for cooking pulses. It is also good for stocks and soups, so if you select recipes carefully you can make really good, quick meals based on peas, beans and lentils. Most pressure cookers are made of aluminium, not a favoured material with health food cooks. It is worth buying one in stainless steel, which will not discolour and which is considered a superior material from the health point of view.

*Vacuum Flask*

Lots of us buy a wide-mouthed vacuum flask and then forget to use it except for keeping food hot on holiday journeys. Yet it can be turned into a valuable ally in the kitchen. The softer pulses may be cooked completely in it, ready for use, while the harder types will soften so that they need far less time to finish off or to incorporate into other dishes. They will 'cook' with absolutely no attention, either overnight or while you are out during the day. You may, of course, prefer the sophistication of the electric slow cooker, particularly if you are well organized and like to prepare a complete dish first thing in the morning. Slow cookers have a very low energy consumption, but the vacuum flask cooks for free.

## Some Super-short Cuts

*Ground Pulses (using electric grinder)*
Wash and pick over peas, beans or lentils and spread them out on tea towels. Pat dry, then change the towels and remove any remaining moisture. If possible, leave spread out for an hour or so, as beans should be completely dry. Put the pulses into the grinder a few spoonsful at a time and reduce to a powder. This may be coarse or fine – the finer it is the less cooking it will need. For freshness of flavour, grind in small quantities. You can, however, keep ground pulses for a week or so in a screw-topped jar, providing they are completely dry.

*To use.* For spreads, *pâtés*, patties, etc. and in soups and stews. To add to soups and stews, take a cupful of the hot stock or cooking liquid and mix with two to three tablespoonsful of ground pulses. Stir this into the pan containing the rest of the ingredients. Stir occasionally or the grains may stick to the bottom of the pan and burn before they are cooked. Do not use too much, as the grains will swell and will thicken the liquid.

If the softer pulses such as lentils are ground dry, they may be cooked very quickly for inclusion in spreads and *pâtés*. Cook them in a little water over low heat, stirring constantly and adding more water as necessary until the individual grains have softened and formed a thick paste. Cool and add to the remaining ingredients.

*Toasted and Ground or Milled Pulses*
I use these methods for chick peas and soya beans, which are among the most useful pulses and rather different in texture from their fellows. Chick peas may be toasted to a mealy texture rather like chestnuts and then milled, whereas the bullet hard soya beans still require the electric grinder after toasting.

*Chick Peas.* Wash, pick over and soak for six to eight hours or overnight, changing the water once or twice if possible. Rinse. Sometimes it is possible to rub handfuls of the peas together at this stage and loosen the skins, which may be discarded. Drain the peas well, spread on tea towels and pat dry. When the oven is in use, spread the chick peas out on baking trays and let them bake at moderate heat for about half an hour or until they have started to split and the insides are soft. Do not let them burn – they should scarcely colour. If you like to live dangerously, soaked chick peas may be toasted under a moderate grill. However, they have a trick of exploding as the skins burst, and the only safe way to grill them is to crush them first to break the skins, a somewhat tedious job.

When the toasted peas are cold, the flesh is too soft to use the electric grinder. Instead, run them through the food mill or 'salad maker', using the drum with small holes. You then have a dry, almost-cooked ingredient with extra flavour from the toasting, which may be used for patties, spreads, etc. without the long cooking usually required for chick peas. When adapting recipes, remember that soaking has already swollen the chick peas to twice their dry weight. The milled toasted peas will keep for a week or so in a screw-topped jar, but it is unlikely that *all* their moisture content has been dried out, so keep the jar in the fridge and use as soon as possible.

*Soya beans.* The hardness of soya beans, frustrating if you try to boil them soft in the ordinary way, becomes an advantage when you toast them. They acquire a good nutty flavour which earns them a place in all manner of dishes, savoury and sweet, even in cakes and breakfast cereals.

This is the method. Wash the beans and soak them for six to eight hours or overnight. Once more, change the water now and again if you can, and leave them in a cool place if the weather is warm or they may begin to ferment. Drain, rinse and drain again. Dry the beans as much as possible on tea towels. Spread them on the grill pan and toast them under moderate heat, shaking the pan now and again so that they brown evenly. About 15 minutes will usually turn them a good, even brown, but it will vary the type and age of the bean.

Spread the toasted beans out to cool, then grind them to powder in the electric grinder. The powder may be coarse or fine, but the finer you make it the more generally useful it proves. It will now have a good, nutty toasted flavour, but this may be emphasized still further if you give the ground beans a second light toasting under the grill. This time you really do have to watch them, as they burn very easily. If the ground beans are quite dry, they will keep for several weeks without refrigeration, but the smallest amount of moisture left in will soon turn them mouldy, so fridge storage is the safest bet. I have given sample recipes for the use of ground toasted soya beans, but you will find that you can add them in small quantities to all manner of dishes – particularly worthwhile in view of their high protein content.

# Weekly Planning

With the methods I have outlined, it is possible to prepare a supply of beans without too much trouble while cooking other foods at the weekend, and then to use them for meals through the week. Another great advantage of bean-based meals is that you can keep several months' dry supplies in the cupboard if you wish. And cooked or prepared beans all ready for use means that you can simply bring in fresh vegetables during the week and have the ingredients for your meal at your fingertips.

For a weekend session of bean cookery, choose several types

of pulses, say soya and chick peas, plus one or two of the similar varieties such as red kidney beans, black eyed, borlotti, etc., or perhaps some butter beans and adzuki for their sweetish flavour. This would give a useful selection for the week of ground toasted soya beans, chick peas ready milled for quick patties etc., and plenty of cooked beans for other dishes. It might also be a good idea to wash some lentils and dry them thoroughly so that they are ready to grind in the coffee grinder for almost-instant soups.

Having achieved a stock of prepared pulses, do not run the risk of having some of them go bad before you can use them. It is not safe to assume that cooked peas and beans will keep for a week at the temperature of the average fridge shelf. If you intend to use them more than three days hence, put them in the freezer or at least in the fridge ice compartment. I find it is best to freeze them in the cooking water (to cover). Drained and frozen for a long period, they tend to dry out – even if well packed.

## Flavouring Pulses

Most pulses do not have a strong flavour. This is both a weakness and a strength – if you serve them 'plain', the family will certainly dub them boring. But their neutral taste means that you can dress them up in all manner of ways.

It is often said that pulses absorb other flavours well. In fact, if you drain beans which have been cooked with herbs and spices, you may well find that they still taste of beans. This applies particularly to harder types such as soya beans. If pulses are cooked to a *purée*, absorbing much of the cooking water, as in the case of lentils and split peas, then they will absorb any added flavours. Otherwise, if you intend to use drained beans, in a salad for example, you need to be fairly heavy handed with the herbs and spices to give a hint of them to the finished result.

*Buying Herbs and Spices*
Many more of us now have access to shops catering chiefly for immigrant families. Not only do they have a fascinating range of spices which are usually cheaper and fresher than those little drums at the supermarket, but they also keep lots of interesting varieties of peas, beans and lentils. You can find good quality garlic there, too, plus fresh ginger root and fresh

coriander. The shopkeepers are friendly, and will explain the uses of the ingredients which may not be familiar, although I must admit to several interesting packets of seasonings in the cupboard about which I am still ignorant! All the curry spices go well with pulses, also chilli, paprika and such things as cinnamon and nutmeg. One beautiful item is fresh ginger root – a thin slice or two is delicious with beans in many soups, stews and mixed vegetable dishes, and especially in stir-fried bean sprouts.

*Home-grown Herbs*
Chopped parsley occurs in many pulse recipes, partly because it goes so well with them and partly because it is the most readily available of the fresh herbs. But lots of other herbs are astonishingly easy to grow. I have little time for gardening, but I have found that sweet basil does well in a pot on a sunny window sill, and that thyme, marjoram, fennel and sage are fairly undemanding. The yeasty flavoured lovage is a great help for stocks and soups (although it grows nine feet tall and takes up a great deal of space) and summer savory, known as the 'bean herb' should also be given a try. The biggest surprise of all is the ease with which fresh coriander will grow in an ordinary garden. Even in a poor summer you can harvest lots of green leaves, and if there is plenty of sunshine you can pick an enormous number of ripe seeds – enough to crush and use through the winter and still leave plenty to replant the following year.

If you have herbs in the garden, do try to keep some for pulse dishes during the sunless months. Home-dried herbs have much more flavour than the shop bought ones – I find that the best method is to stretch a piece of old net curtaining with an open weave over a slatted wooden fruit tray. Herbs spread out on this will dry nicely in the airing cupboard and may then be crumbled into jars for the winter. Frozen herbs are sometimes even better. They do go limp when thawed out, and you will not get the effect of fresh chopped herbs, but the flavour is often far better than that of dried herbs. Simply pick sprigs or leaves and freeze them in small quantities in bags or tubs. Basil is one of the best – the flavour stays true although the leaves discolour. Mint and lovage are also very good.

*Stocks and Other Flavourings*

Pulses may, of course, be cooked in plain water, and this is perfectly satisfactory if you intend to add them to other dishes afterwards. But when making soups, stews, etc., where the peas and beans are cooked with other ingredients, the flavour of the finished dish is greatly improved by using a good stock. It is even more helpful when cooking lentils or split peas, which will absorb the cooking liquid. I have given a method for making vegetable stock on p.28. For the occasions when I am in a hurry and there is no stock on hand I use Hugli vegetable stock cubes from the health food store.

Oranges and lemons – both rind and juice – are delicious with pulses, and it is possible to use flavour which would otherwise be wasted by using the skins to make dried fruit rind. Wash orange or lemon skins in several changes of boiling water and let them dry. Peel off very thin strips of skin without taking any of the white pith, put them on baking trays and let them dry out in a very slow heat over several days whenever the oven is in use. When they are brittle and completely dry, crush them and store in small airtight containers. Lemon juice is one of the best additions to finished dishes if you feel that the taste tends to be rather bland. I would also not be without canned tomato *purée* which will strengthen the flavour of most soups and stews.

# Bean Sprouts

Until recently, most of us only met with bean sprouts when eating in Chinese restaurants, but it is now fashionable to grow them in the kitchen. You can sprout most beans and seeds, but some have a lower germination rate than others. They should, of course, be unsprayed crops, preferably sold for sprouting, and they need to be fairly fresh, too, to be really successful.

It has to be said that sprouting beans is not an occupation for those who are frequently out of the house, as they have to be rinsed several times a day to keep them fresh and sweet. If you were away for the weekend, you would need to detail a bean sitter to keep an eye on them!

Mung beans are undoubtedly the best for sprouting, germinating fairly reliably and producing crunchy sprouts which are good cooked or raw. The jar method is by far the simplest. Rinse the beans in cold water, soak them overnight, rinse them again and put them in a large glass jar. Fix a piece of muslin or open weave nylon over the top with a rubber band. Drain out all the water and keep the jar on its side in a moderately warm place, tipped slightly so that any moisture drains towards the opening. If you keep the sides of the jar covered with a cloth, the sprouts will stay white. Rinse and drain three times a day, swilling the water round and draining very gently once the sprouts begin to appear, otherwise you may break them. Use the sprouts when they are about $\frac{3}{4}$ inch long, or stop their growth by refrigerating them and use within a couple of days.

Home-produced bean sprouts rarely come up as thick and succulent as those you can buy, but they do have the advantage of being really fresh. Bean sprouts may now be bought in some greengrocers and supermarkets and in the excellent food departments of a well known chain store. The chain store sprouts (sold in film covered packs) are extremely good and if you buy them loose at the greengrocers you can inspect the condition. But never try to keep bought bean sprouts for longer than a day. Pre-packs in supermarkets are sometimes already stale and will go rotten very quickly.

## Pulses on the Menu

Budgeting and cooking for family meals these days can be a thankless task. Odds are that if you cook for four people, you have at least one who will inform you in no uncertain terms that he or she does not like beans. I would suggest, however, that if you keep quiet and keep the packets hidden, even the most vocal bean hater can be fed valuable amounts of pulses without being any the wiser. Soups may be liquidized, ground lentils disappear into casseroles, mashed butter beans combined innocuously with cream cheese, and so on. Toasted soya beans in breakfast cereals are notable only for their crunchiness. And those in the family who do like beans can only be surprised at the number of ways they may be used.

When trying out a new recipe it is usually advisable to make a small quantity first to see how you like it – I learned this the hard way many years ago as a new cook! Small quantities can also be teamed up with other dishes, and I feel that many bean recipes are best eaten in this way, as part of a meal composed of several dishes. Bean salads, for instance, can form part of a mixed salad platter, bean patties are good preceded by a mixed vegetable soup or accompanied by a rice or potato dish and a green salad.

I have also come to the conclusion that one family's idea of a snack is another family's main meal, and for that reason the number of servings given should be taken as a guide only – they depend upon the way in which you want to use the recipes and to plan your menus.

Most pulses double their weight when soaked, and retain this weight when cooked. I have given weights for *cooked* beans in recipes which are likely to be made from beans already cooked in quantity and kept in the fridge or freezer.

# 1
# BASIC RECIPES

This chapter gives the recipes for stocks, sauces, salad dressings and pastry that I have found go well with pulses. If you like making large quantities for future use, you will find that the tomato sauce freezes very well and that the pastry doughs may be frozen, either baked or unbaked. The pastry doughs, unlike those made with white flour, will discolour if kept in the fridge for more than two or three days. It is better to keep the rubbed-in mixture in a covered box in the fridge and to take out the amount you need each time and add the liquid. Cooked pancakes freeze well – let them come back to room temperature and then reheat them between two plates over hot water.

I must confess that I prefer to use 81 per cent flour for pastry and use wholemeal flour for cakes and breads. If using wholemeal flour, handle the dough as little as possible, using a fork for most of the mixing. If the pastry tends to break up in rolling, flour it lightly and roll between two sheets of greaseproof paper.

# Vegetable Stock

**2 sticks celery, with leaves
1 onion
1 clove garlic
1 carrot
6 peppercorns
6 stalks parsley
2-3 sprigs thyme** *or*
**½ teaspoonful dried thyme** *or*
**other herbs, e.g. savory, lovage, rosemary
3 pts (1.5 litres) water**

Wash celery and break up roughly. Peel and halve the onion and garlic. Scrape carrot and cut into thick pieces. Put vegetables and herbs in a large pan with the water, bring to the boil and simmer for about 45 minutes. Strain.

## Double Strength Stock

Make as above, then boil the strained stock for about 30 minutes, or until reduced by half.

## Yeast and Vegetable Stock

Make either single- or double-strength stock and add a little yeast extract, being careful not to make the stock too salty.

# Basic White Sauce

**1 oz (25g) butter or margarine**
**1 oz (25g) 81 per cent plain flour**
**½ pt (275ml) milk**
**Sea-salt**
**Freshly-ground black pepper**

Melt the butter in a small pan, stir in the flour off the heat and then cook together for a few minutes, stirring. Gradually blend in the milk, stirring well to avoid lumps, bring to the boil and simmer gently until thickened. Season to taste. Alternatively, place the butter, flour and milk all in the pan together and bring slowly to the boil, whisking or stirring constantly, until thick.

## Vegetable Flavoured Sauce

If you are making white sauce to serve with a strongly flavoured vegetable such as onion, leek or cauliflower, cook the vegetable first and keep hot, reserving the cooking water. Use this half–and–half with milk to make the sauce.

## Cheese Sauce

Add 2-3 oz (50-75g) grated cheese to basic white sauce or vegetable flavoured sauce with extra seasoning if you wish, such as a pinch of dry mustard or paprika.

# Parsley Sauce

$\frac{1}{2}$ pt (275ml) milk
$\frac{1}{4}$ pt (150ml) vegetable stock (see p.28)
1$\frac{1}{2}$ oz (40g) butter
1 oz (25g) wholemeal flour
1 teaspoonful lemon juice
3 tablespoonsful finely chopped parsley
1 teaspoonful ground coriander
Pinch cayenne pepper
Sea-salt
Freshly-ground black pepper

Put the milk, vegetable stock, butter and flour in a saucepan and whisk together over moderate heat until smooth and thick. Cook for a further five minutes, stirring constantly with a wooden spoon. Add lemon juice, parsley and coriander and season with cayenne, salt and pepper.

# Tomato Sauce

**1 small onion**
**1 clove garlic**
**1 tablespoonful vegetable oil**
**14 oz (400g) can tomatoes**
**1 bay leaf**
**2-3 parsley stalks**
**3-4 leaves fresh basil** *or*
**1 teaspoonful dried thyme or marjoram**
**Sea-salt**
**Freshly-ground black pepper**
**Dash sherry (optional)**

Peel and chop onion. Peel and crush garlic. Fry gently together in the oil until beginning to soften. Do not brown. Add tomatoes and herbs and season with salt and pepper. Add sherry if you wish.

Bring to the boil, lower the heat and simmer for about 20 minutes or until the sauce is thick. If it thickens too much, add a little water during cooking. If not for immediate use, cool the sauce and refrigerate or freeze in a covered container.

# Chilli Tomato Sauce

2 medium onions
2 large cloves garlic
Vegetable oil
1¾ lb (800g) can tomatoes
1-inch (2.5cm) piece fresh ginger root, peeled and
chopped
4 slices lemon
4 tablespoonsful cider vinegar
2 tablespoonsful soft, brown sugar
2 bay leaves
3-4 parsley stalks
1 teaspoonful dried thyme or marjoram
½ pt (275ml) water
2 teaspoonsful sea-salt
2 sticks celery, roughly chopped
2 tablespoonsful Holbrooks vegetarian sauce
3 teaspoonsful chilli sauce (or to taste)
1 tablespoonful tomato *purée*

Peel and chop onions and garlic and fry gently in a little
oil until beginning to soften. Turn into a saucepan and
add all remaining ingredients except the chilli sauce and
tomato *purée*.

Bring to the boil and simmer for about 30 minutes.
Strain, pressing to extract flavour from the vegetables.
Return strained sauce to the pan, bring to the boil and
simmer until reduced by about one third. Add chilli
sauce to taste and tomato *purée*.

Cool, store in fridge and use as required, or divide
between several small containers and freeze for longer
storage.

# Guacamole Sauce

**2 very ripe avocado pears**
**4 ripe tomatoes**
**1 medium onion**
**1 medium green pepper**
**1 tablespoonful chopped parsley**
**1 teaspoonful sea-salt**
**½ teaspoonful freshly-ground black pepper**

Halve the avocados and remove the stones. Scoop out the flesh and mash it well with a wooden spoon. Skin and chop the tomatoes. Peel and chop the onion. Wash and de-seed the pepper and chop it finely. Mix all the ingredients together and season well.

# Sweet and Sour Sauce

**1 medium onion**
**3 tablespoonful vegetable oil**
**2 teaspoonsful grated fresh ginger root**
**¼ pt (150ml) wine or cider vinegar**
**2 tablespoonful honey**
**1 tablespoonful soft brown sugar**
**1 tablespoonful cornflour**
**1 tablespoonful soya sauce**
**Dash of sherry (optional)**

Peel the onion and slice thinly. Fry in the oil over moderate heat for about three minutes, stirring occasionally. Add the grated ginger and fry for two to three minutes. Take off the heat and stir in the vinegar, honey, sugar and about half a teacupful of water.

Bring slowly to the boil, stirring to dissolve the sugar. Mix the cornflour and soya sauce to a paste with a little more water and add to the pan. Stir constantly until the sauce thickens. This sauce is usually served with the onions left in it, but may be strained if you prefer a clear sauce. Add sherry just before serving.

# French Dressing

⅔ pt (400ml) olive or corn oil
⅓ pt (200ml) wine or cider vinegar
1-2 tablespoonsful lemon juice
Sea-salt
Freshly-ground black pepper
Pinch dry mustard
Pinch light soft brown sugar

Mix all ingredients in a screw-topped jar and shake well.
Taste and add more salt or sugar if needed.

*Variations*
*Garlic.* Cut a clove of garlic in two and steep it in the
dressing overnight. Remove before use.
  *Honey.* Use clear honey as a sweetener and omit the
mustard.

# Yogurt Dressing

5 fl oz (150ml) natural yogurt
2 tablespoonsful corn oil
Juice of 1 lemon
Sea-salt
Paprika

Mix the yogurt with the oil and lemon juice. Season with
salt and a pinch of paprika.

## Quick Mayonnaise

**4 tablespoonsful white wine vinegar**
**1 small egg**
**½ teaspoonful light, soft, brown sugar or honey**
**¼ teaspoonful sea-salt**
**¾ pt (425ml) olive oil**

Place all ingredients except oil in the liquidizer goblet.
Blend, then add the oil very gradually with the machine
running. Continue blending until thickened. Adjust
seasoning. To make the mayonnaise thicker, add a little
more oil and continue blending.

## Lemon Cream Dressing

**4 tablespoonsful double cream**
**4 tablespoonsful mayonnaise**
**Grated rind of 1 lemon**
**Juice of ¼ lemon, or to taste**
**Good pinch dry mustard**
**Sea-salt**
**Freshly-ground black pepper**

Put the cream in a basin and whisk until thickened but
not too stiff. Mix with mayonnaise. Add the grated outer
rind of the lemon, being careful not to take any of the
white pith. Gradually work in about a tablespoonful of
lemon juice and add mustard, salt and pepper. Taste and
add more lemon juice if needed.

This is best when freshly made, but left-over dressing
may be stored for the following day in the fridge, in a
covered container.

*Quick Mayonnaise*

# Flaky Pastry

**8 oz (225g) 81 per cent plain flour**
**Pinch sea-salt**
**5-6 oz (150-175g) margarine**
**Ice-cold water to mix**

Mix flour and salt. Divide the margarine into three portions. Rub one portion into the flour in the usual way and mix to a stiff dough with a little cold water. Roll out into an oblong.

Take the second portion of fat, cut it into small pieces and dot it over two-thirds of the dough. Dust with flour and fold the dough in three. Turn the pastry at right angles and lightly indent it at intervals with the rolling pin (this helps to make it rise evenly). Seal the open ends.

Leave in a cool place for 15 minutes, then roll out and repeat the process with the remaining fat. Rest and roll the dough again, sealing the ends. If the paste becomes too soft and sticky, let it firm up in the fridge before re-rolling.

# Quick Flaky Pastry

**8 oz (225g) 81 per cent plain flour**
**Pinch sea-salt**
**6 oz (175g) margarine, very cold**
**Ice-cold water to mix**

Mix flour and salt. To make this pastry successfully, the margarine needs to be really hard, preferably firmed up in the ice-box for a while before use. Pull back the wrapper and mark off 6 oz (175g) lightly with a knife. Using a coarse grater, grate the margarine into the flour, working towards the mark. Distribute it through the flour with a fork. Add enough cold water to make a firm dough, mixing as much as possible with a fork so that the margarine does not soften too much. Form into a ball, flour and leave in a cool place for 15 minutes before rolling out in the usual way.

This pastry is slightly less flaky than that produced by the previous recipe, but it makes a very acceptable alternative when time is short. Best eaten hot.

# Shortcrust Pastry

**8 oz (225g) 81 per cent plain flour**
**½ teaspoonful sea-salt**
**4 oz (100g) margarine** *or*
**2 oz (50g) margarine** *and*
**2 oz (50g) white vegetable fat**
**Cold water to mix**

Mix flour and salt and rub in the fat until mixture resembles breadcrumbs. Add about four tablespoonsful of cold water and mix to a firm dough. Use just enough water to hold the pastry together for rolling. If possible, cover or wrap in food film and leave in a cool place for 15-30 minutes before rolling out. In hot weather, refrigerate lightly, but do not let the dough become too hard.

# Sweet Shortcrust

**8 oz (225g) 81 per cent self-raising flour**
**½ teaspoonful sea-salt**
**4 oz (100g) margarine** *or*
**2 oz (50g) margarine** *and*
**2 oz (50g) white vegetable fat**
**1 dessertspoonful light, soft, brown sugar**
**4 tablespoonsful milk**

Mix flour and salt and rub in the fats until mixture resembles breadcrumbs. Stir sugar into the milk and dissolve as much as possible. Use this sweetened milk to mix the dough, adding a little more milk if necessary. If possible, leave in a cool place for a short while, before rolling out.

# Pancakes

**4 oz (100g) 81 per cent plain flour**
**Pinch sea-salt**
**1 egg and 1 yolk**
**½ pt (275ml) milk**
**1 tablespoonful vegetable oil**

Mix flour and salt. Make a well in the centre and drop in the egg and the yolk. Add a little milk and draw the flour in gradually, stirring well with a wooden spoon and adding more milk as you need it. Add the oil and the rest of the milk. Now beat the batter thoroughly and leave, covered, for two to three hours. Beat again before use and add a little cold water if it has thickened up too much. This quantity will make about 15 thin 6-inch (15cm) pancakes – fewer, of course, if you make the thick pancakes which some families prefer.

# 2
# SOUPS AND SNACKS

Meal patterns these days have to be flexible and many of us simply do not have the time to make every meal a sit-down, three course affair. If you have a good bowl of bean-based soup in the fridge or freezer you are halfway to a really nourishing light meal, however impromptu it may seem!

Other useful fridge standbys include spreads made from pulses. For the more elegant, premeditated snacks to hand round when friends call, try pastry tartlets and deep-fried savouries.

When time is desperately short, there are even quicker dishes in the Fast Food section beginning on p.55.

# Lentil and Mushroom Soup

It would be hard to find a soup using less fuel than this one – it cooks quietly by itself in a vacuum jar without any attention at all. Just add seasoning and fresh herbs and serve with toast or *croûtons*.

**2 oz (50g) continental lentils**
**1 medium onion**
**1 clove garlic**
**2 oz (50g) mushrooms**
**½ oz (15g) butter**
**½ teaspoonful coriander seeds**
**½-inch (1cm) piece fresh ginger root**
**1 pt (575ml) vegetable stock (see p.28)**
**2 teaspoonsful frozen orange juice concentrate**
**Sea-salt**
**Freshly-ground black pepper**
**2-3 tablespoonsful chopped parsley**
**2 teaspoonsful chopped, fresh coriander (optional)**

Pick over the lentils and wash well. Drain, turn into a basin and cover with boiling water while preparing the vegetables. Check that your vacuum jar will take approximately 1½ pts (850ml) water, leaving a space below the stopper. Fill it with hot water. Peel and chop onion and garlic. Wash, dry and slice the mushrooms. Fry together in the butter over moderate heat until beginning to soften.

Crush the coriander seeds, peel and chop the ginger root and add to the pan. Turn up the heat and fry briskly for two to three minutes, stirring constantly. Drain the lentils and add to the pan with the stock and orange juice concentrate. Bring to the boil, stirring. Empty the vacuum jar and pour in the soup, making sure that there is an inch or so of air space at the top. Close the jar and leave for 6-8 hours.

Transfer the soup to a saucepan, reheat and season to taste with salt and pepper. Stir in chopped parsley before serving. Fresh coriander may also be added if available.
Serves 2-3.

# Minestrone

A true 'complete meal' soup – serve it with plenty of grated cheese and a green salad.

**4 oz (100g) haricot or red kidney beans**
**1 large onion**
**1 clove garlic**
**2 tablespoonsful vegetable oil**
**Vegetable stock (see p.28)**
**Sea-salt to taste**
**Freshly-ground black pepper**
**2 large stalks celery**
**2 carrots**
**3-4 tomatoes**
**2 oz (50g) wholemeal macaroni or**
**Broken spaghetti**
**6 oz (175g) firm white cabbage**

Soak the beans overnight in plenty of water. Drain and rinse beans, then drain again. Peel and chop the onion. Peel and crush the garlic. Fry together in oil until beginning to brown. Transfer to a heavy saucepan and add the beans and about $2\frac{1}{2}$ pts (1·25 litres) vegetable stock. Bring to the boil, then simmer gently until the beans are cooked. Add salt and pepper to taste.

While the beans are cooking, wash and chop the celery and carrots. Skin and chop the tomatoes. Add to the pan and cook for about 20 minutes. Towards the end of cooking time, add the pasta and finally shred the cabbage and cook until tender but still crisp. Adjust seasoning before serving.

Serves 4.

# Celery and Lentil Soup

Another 'quickie' using ground pulses. Serve with plenty of fresh herbs chopped in before serving.

**1 small head celery**
**1 medium onion**
**1 large potato**
**1 oz (25g) butter**
**1 tablespoonful vegetable oil**
**1½ pts (850ml) vegetable stock (see p.28)**
**2 rounded tablespoonsful ground lentils (see p.19)**
**Sea-salt**
**Freshly-ground black pepper**
**Small sprig fresh tarragon** *or*
**½ teaspoonful dried tarragon**
**Chopped parsley**
**Chopped chives or other fresh herbs**

Scrub celery well and discard any damaged pieces, but retain the leaves. Chop roughly. Peel and chop the onion and potato. Cook gently together in butter and oil in a heavy pan, covered, until the vegetables begin to soften. Stir occasionally.

Mix ground lentils with a little of the stock in a cup. Add to the pan with remaining stock, tarragon and seasoning. Bring to the boil and simmer for about ten minutes, stirring occasionally.

Cool, transfer to liquidizer and reduce to a *purée*. Return to the pan, rubbing through a coarse sieve to remove the celery strings. Return to the boil, adjust seasoning and sprinkle with plenty of chopped parsley and other herbs as available.

Serves 3-4.

# Curried Lentil Soup

A thick, substantial soup. If you prefer, add more water and liquidize, but it is very good with the fried onion added at the end.

**6 oz (175g) red or yellow lentils**
**½ teaspoonful curry powder**
**¼ teaspoonful turmeric**
**2 teaspoonsful sea-salt, or to taste**
**2 bay leaves**
**1 medium onion**
**1 teaspoonful freshly-grated ginger root**
**2 tablespoonsful vegetable oil**
**Garam masala**

Pick over the lentils and wash well. Place in a strong saucepan with about 1¼ pts (725ml) water, the curry powder, turmeric, salt and bay leaves and bring to the boil. Turn heat down and simmer gently, covered, for about 45 minutes or until lentils are soft.

Peel and slice the onion and fry with the grated ginger in the oil until the onion is golden brown. Mix into the soup, check seasoning and sprinkle with garam masala before serving.

Serves 2-3.

# Bean and Watercress Soup

Green soups make a fresh looking and attractive change in the winter months – this one uses tangy watercress and white beans for a good colour.

**1 large onion**
**1 oz (25g) butter**
**1 tablespoonful 81 per cent plain flour**
**2 sticks celery**
**1 bunch watercress**
**6 oz (175g) cooked butter beans**
**Sea-salt**
**Milk or single cream**

Peel and chop onion and fry gently in the butter until beginning to soften. Do not brown. Mix in the flour and cook, stirring, for two to three minutes. Scrub celery, chop roughly and add to the pan. Stir in about 1¼ pts (725ml) hot water, season lightly with salt and bring to the boil. Simmer until the celery is soft, then add the well-washed watercress and the butter beans and cook for a few minutes until the watercress is limp.

Cool slightly, turn into liquidizer goblet and reduce to a *purée*. Return to the pan, rubbing through a coarse sieve. Add milk or cream to taste, reheat gently and check seasoning.

Serves 3-4.

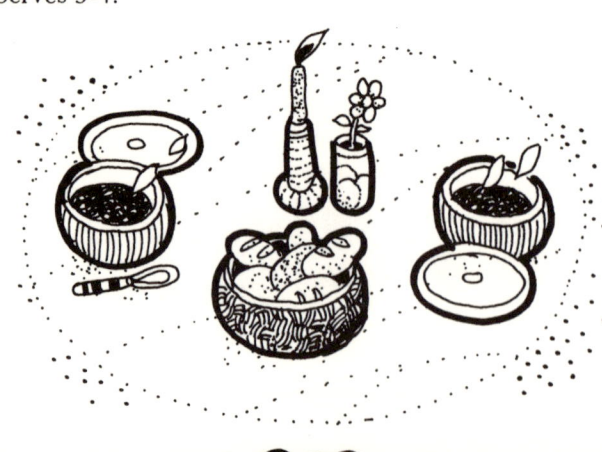

## Chilled Summer Soup

Here is another green soup, this time cool and minty for the summer.

1 cucumber
1 small onion
1 oz (25g) butter
2 rounded tablespoonsful ground, green split peas
¾ pt (425ml) vegetable stock (see p.28)
½ pt (275ml) milk
2 tablespoonsful chopped mint
1 carton soured cream
Sea-salt
White pepper
Mint sprigs to garnish

Peel and chop the cucumber. Peel and chop the onion and cook gently in the butter in a large saucepan until soft. Blend the ground split peas with a little of the stock and add to the pan with the rest of the stock, half the milk and the chopped mint and cucumber. Bring to the boil, cover and simmer gently for 15 minutes. Cool. Reduce to a smooth *purée* in the liquidizer. Stir in the rest of the milk and the soured cream and season to taste. Chill well and garnish with sprigs of mint before serving.
  Serves 3-4.

## Croûtons

Trim the crusts from thick slices of wholemeal bread, preferably slightly dry, and cut into small squares. Fry over moderate heat in a mixture of half oil, half butter until crisp and brown, turning once. Drain on kitchen paper and keep hot until required. Ready-fried *croûtons* may be frozen and reheated in a moderate oven.

## Oven-Baked Croûtons

To make a large quantity, heat oil and butter in a baking tin in a fairly hot oven, arrange the bread squares carefully in the hot fat and bake until crisp, turning once. A batch of *croûtons* may be made in this way when the oven is in use for other dishes, and then frozen for future use.

## Cheese Dumplings

**1 oz (25g) wholemeal self-raising flour**
**1 oz (25g) wholemeal breadcrumbs**
**1 teaspoonful baking powder**
**1 oz (25g) margarine**
**3 oz (75g) grated cheese, preferably dry**
**Sea-salt**
**Freshly-ground black pepper**
**1 small egg**

Mix together the flour, breadcrumbs, baking powder, salt and pepper. Rub in the margarine and mix in the cheese. Beat the egg in a cup and add enough to the dry ingredients to make a stiff dough. Roll into tiny dumplings, place carefully in the soup and simmer, covered, for about 15 minutes.

## Cheese or Curry Fingers

Trim the crusts from dry wholemeal bread and spread the slices thinly with butter. Sprinkle generously with grated cheese, or lightly with curry powder. Cut into fingers and toast under the grill, or place on a baking sheet and brown in a hot oven.

# Creamy Cheese Spread

Butter beans combine beautifully with cream cheese and you can flavour the spread in lots of different ways. Use it for sandwiches, or with crispbreads, rolls or crackers.

**4 oz (100g) cooked butter beans**
**2 oz (50g) cream cheese**
**Sea-salt to taste**

Mill the butter beans or mash well, removing skins where possible. Soften the cream cheese with a fork, add the mashed beans and beat well together, seasoning with salt to taste.

*Variations*

*Curry and pineapple.* Add a good pinch of curry powder and 2-3 canned pineapple rings, well-drained and chopped.

*Herbs.* Beat in 2-3 tablespoonsful finely chopped herbs, such as a mixture of chives and parsley.

*Tomato and garlic.* Rub a small serving bowl well with a cut clove of garlic. Beat the mashed beans and cheese together in the bowl and gradually beat in about 1 tablespoonful tomato *purée*, or more to taste.

# Buttery Herb Spread

A useful recipe for the summer months – fresh mint and parsley combined with flageolets make an attractive green spread for sandwiches or crackers. Frozen mint leaves may be used in the winter.

**4 oz (100g) flageolets**
**2 oz (50g) butter**
**Sea-salt**
**2-3 tablespoonsful chopped parsley**
**2-3 tablespoonsful chopped mint**
**Small clove garlic (optional)**

Soak and cook flageolets. Drain and mash well or make into a *purée* in the liquidizer with a little of the cooking water but do not make the mixture too wet. The *purée* may be rubbed through a coarse sieve if you prefer a smoother spread.

When the *purée* is cold, beat in the butter and add salt to taste. Work the herbs in gradually, tasting until the flavour of mint is strong enough without being overpowering. Garlic may be added by rubbing a cut clove round the bowl before mixing the spread or by skinning the clove, crushing it thoroughly and beating it into the spread.

Serve with crusty bread, wholemeal crackers or crispbread.

# Savoury Stuffed Apples

Serve hot or cold, one for each person as a starter or two each for a light lunch.

**4 oz (100g) yellow split peas**
**1 medium onion**
**1 tablespoonful vegetable oil**
**1 teaspoonful ground cinnamon**
**2 tablespoonsful finely chopped celery**
**1 oz (25g) walnuts, finely milled**
**Sea-salt to taste**
**2 oz (50g) butter**
**4 large cooking apples**
**1 oz (25g) soft, brown sugar**
**1 tablespoonful wine or cider vinegar**

To make the filling, pick over the split peas, wash well and boil or pressure cook (see p.18) until soft. Drain well. Peel the onion, chop finely and fry gently in the oil until soft but not brown. Add the cinnamon, chopped celery and walnuts, salt to taste and half the butter.

Wash apples well and carefully remove the cores without cutting right through to the base. Cut out some of the pulp as well to make room for the stuffing. Chop the pulp which has been removed and add it to the split pea mixture. Pack the stuffing into the apples, mounding it slightly if necessary. With a sharp knife, make a cut round the circumference of the apples about half-way down to prevent bursting.

Arrange apples in a baking dish, dot with remaining butter and add about half an inch of water to the dish together with the vinegar and sugar. Bake at 325°F/170°C (Gas Mark 3) for about 1 hour or until apples are tender, basting frequently and adding more water during cooking if necessary.

# Jiffy Pizza

A quick and tasty way of using up left-over cooked beans and tomato sauce is to make pizza in individual pie plates and use a scone dough base. Use any kind of beans you have on hand and experiment with other herb and vegetable toppings.

**8 oz (225g) 81 per cent self-raising flour**
**½ teaspoonful sea-salt**
**3 tablespoonsful vegetable oil**
**6 tablespoonsful milk**
**8 oz (225g) cooked beans, any type**
**3 oz (75g) mushrooms**
**½ oz (15g) butter**
**¼ medium green pepper**
**8-10 tablespoonsful tomato sauce (see p.31)**
**3-4 tablespoonsful chopped basil**
**4 oz (100g) grated cheese**

Mix the flour and salt, add the oil and milk and mix quickly to a soft dough. Another spoonful of milk may be added if needed, but do not make the mixture too wet. Divide the dough in four, roll out lightly and line four individual foil pie plates about 6 inches (15cm) across.

Divide the cooked beans between the pastry cases. Wash, dry and slice the mushrooms and cook quickly in the butter until soft. De-seed the pepper and cut into thin rings or strips. Arrange the mushrooms and peppers on top of the beans and cover with tomato sauce. Sprinkle with the chopped basil and finish with the grated cheese.

Bake at 425°F/220°C (Gas Mark 7) for about 15 minutes, or until the pastry is lightly browned and the cheese bubbling.

Makes 4.

*Variation*

Fill the pastry cases with left-over chilli beans (see p.107) and top with tomato sauce. Omit the other vegetables and the grated cheese.

# Chick Pea Savoury Tartlets

These tasty little savouries may be served in a variety of ways, as a snack with drinks or as a light meal. Try them hot with onion or tomato sauce, green salad and rice, or cold with a sharply dressed watercress, celery and apple salad.

**Flaky pastry made with 8 oz (225g) flour (see p.36)**
**1 medium leek**
**1 medium onion**
**4 large black olives**
**2 tablespoonsful chopped parsley**
**1 egg**
**2 tablespoonsful wholemeal flour**
**½ teaspoonful ground mace**
**¼ teaspoonful sea-salt**
**4 oz (100g) chick peas, ground (see p.20)**
**¾ pt (425ml) vegetable stock (see p.28)**

Roll out pastry and line small tartlet or patty tins. Trim and wash the leek, peel and chop onion, stone and chop olives. Put into the liquidizer goblet with the parsley, egg, flour, mace and salt. Run the machine at high speed for about 20 seconds or until the mixture is well blended. Turn into a bowl and reserve.

Put the ground chick peas into a saucepan and gradually stir in the stock to make a smooth, creamy mixture. Bring slowly to the boil, stirring well, then turn down the heat, half-cover the pan and simmer gently for ten minutes, stirring occasionally. Cool slightly, then add to the egg and vegetable mixture and mix well.

Fill the pastry cases and bake at 450°F/230°C (Gas Mark 8) for ten minutes, then reduce heat to 375°F/190°C (Gas Mark 5) for a further ten minutes or until filling is cooked and lightly browned.

Makes about 18.

# Deep-Fried Savoury Puffs

A delicious way of using up left-over white sauce and small amounts of pastry with almost any type of cooked beans. Make up the savouries and put them in the fridge, covered, until you are ready to fry them – but be sure to let them come back to room temperature before cooking. Serve as a snack with drinks, or with salad for a light lunch.

**Flaky or 'quick flaky' pastry made with 4 oz (100g)
flour (see pp.36/37)
1½ oz (40g) cream cheese
3 tablespoonsful white sauce (see p.29)
3 oz (75g) cooked beans (red kidney, adzuki, black,
borlotti)
1½ oz (40g) cooked unpolished rice
2 teaspoonsful chopped parsley
Sea-salt
½ teaspoonful grated lemon rind, or to taste
Good pinch curry powder**

Roll out the pastry thinly and cut 3-inch (8cm) circles with a fluted cutter. Roll each one again lightly so that they become slightly larger and really thin. Mix the cream cheese thoroughly with the white sauce. If the beans are large chop or mash them roughly and add to the sauce with the rice and parsley. Season to taste with salt, lemon rind and curry powder.

Place a good teaspoonful of filling on half of each pastry circle. Fold over and seal, crimping the edges securely, to make miniature turnovers. Fry a few at a time in deep hot fat for about five minutes or until brown and crisp. Drain on kitchen paper and keep hot on a serving dish while frying the remaining batches.

Makes about 12.

# 3
# FAST FOOD

Ten-minute soup from pulses may sound incredible but try it anyway! Some of these quick recipes do depend on using kitchen gadgets (see pages 14-19), but if you are a cook who works outside the home, you have probably decided already that gadgets more than earn their keep. I have also included some recipes which are based on ready-cooked beans – extra quantities prepared when you have time can be life-savers when you come in tired and need a swiftly made meal.

# Onion and Lentil Soup

Good with crisply fried *croûtons* or with toast fingers.

**12 oz (350g) onions**
**8 oz (225g) potatoes**
**1 oz (25g) butter**
**1 oz (25g) split red lentils, ground (see p.19)**
**2 pts (1 litre) vegetable stock (see p.28)**
**Sea-salt**
**Freshly-ground black pepper**

Peel and chop the onions and potatoes. Melt butter in a heavy pan and cook vegetables, covered, over low heat for about ten minutes or until beginning to soften. Add ground lentils and stock. Bring to the boil and simmer for 15 minutes.

Cool slightly, then blend to a smooth *purée* in the liquidizer. Return soup to the pan, season well with salt and pepper and gently heat through.

Serves 4.

# Beanpot Soup

A substantial soup for supper with the help of the pressure cooker – it takes less than 45 minutes from the time you open the kitchen door. Serve with crusty bread or *croûtons* and lots of grated cheese.

**3 oz (75g) borlotti or pinto beans**
**2 sticks celery**
**2 carrots**
**1 medium leek**
**1 medium onion**
**1 clove garlic**
**½ oz (15g) butter**
**10 oz (275g) potatoes**
**2 pts (1 litre) vegetable stock**
**2 tablespoonsful tomato** *purée*
**Sea-salt**
**Freshly-ground black pepper**
**2 teaspoonsful lemon juice, or to taste**
**3 tablespoonsful chopped parsley**

Pick over the beans, wash well and soak for ten minutes in boiling water. Wash, scrape and chop the carrots and celery. Trim leek, split, wash well and chop. Peel and chop onion and garlic. Melt butter in the pressure cooker and fry vegetables gently while the beans are soaking.

Peel potatoes and slice very thinly. Drain beans, rinse and add to the cooker with the sliced potatoes and stock. Close the cooker, bring to pressure and cook for 25 minutes. Reduce pressure and remove lid.

Cool for a few minutes, then mash the soup with a slotted spoon or potato masher to break up the cooked potato which will thicken the liquid. Stir in the tomato *purée* and season well with salt and pepper. Add lemon juice to taste, reheat and serve sprinkled with the chopped parsley.

Serves 3-4.

# Creamy Curried Soup

This is a delicately flavoured soup. Quickly made, it is subtle enough for guests to think you have spent hours preparing it. Add just a little curry at first and another pinch or so at the end of cooking.

4 oz (100g) onion, (peeled weight)
4 oz (100g) parsnip (peeled weight)
1 oz (25g) butter
2 rounded tablespoonsful ground field beans (see p.19)
1½ pts (850ml) vegetable stock (see p.28)
Sea-salt
Freshly-ground black pepper
¼ teaspoonful curry powder, or to taste
3-4 tablespoonsful single cream
2-3 sprigs watercress, roughly chopped, to garnish

Peel and slice the onion. Quarter the parsnip and remove the hard centre. Cut parsnip into small pieces. Melt the butter in a large saucepan and cook the onion and parsnip, covered, over moderate heat, for about ten minutes or until beginning to soften.

Mix the ground beans with a teacupful of stock. Add to the pan with the rest of the stock and season with salt, pepper and curry powder. Bring to the boil and simmer for 15 minutes. Cool slightly, transfer to the liquidizer and reduce to a smooth *purée*. Return to the pan, reheat and adjust seasoning.

Stir a spoonful of cream lightly into each helping of soup and garnish with a little chopped watercress.

Serves 3-4.

# Ten-Minute Soup

A hearty and restorative soup – a good standby for the evenings when you come in tired and do not feel at all like cooking.

**2 oz (50g) red kidney beans, ground (see p.19)**
**1½ pts (850ml) vegetable stock (see p.28)**
**4 oz (100g) potato**
**4 oz (100g) onions**
**Sea-salt**
**Freshly-ground black pepper**
**Lemon juice**
**Chopped parsley or chives**
**Wholemeal toast fingers**

Place the ground beans in the pressure cooker with the stock. Peel and roughly chop the potato and onion and add to the pan. Stir to distribute the ground beans, then close the cooker, bring to pressure and cook for ten minutes.

Cool the soup, liquidize and return to the cooker. Season to taste with salt, pepper and lemon juice and serve piping hot with toast fingers.

Serves 3.

# Leek and Broad Bean Soup

Dried broad beans have a distinctive flavour, but they take a long time to cook and the skins can be tough. Using them this way, you can have the flavour without the fuss.

**4 oz (100g) dried broad beans, ground (see p.19)**
**2 tablespoonsful vegetable oil**
**1½ pts (850ml) water**
**8 oz (225g) potato**
**3 leeks**
**2 cloves garlic**
**Sea-salt**
**Freshly-ground black pepper**
**Cream or top of milk**

Place the ground beans in the pressure cooker with the oil and water. Peel potatoes and chop roughly. Trim and split leeks and wash well. Cut up and add to the pan with the peeled cloves of garlic.

Close the pan, bring to pressure and cook for ten minutes. Cool the soup, liquidize and return to the pan. Season to taste and stir in enough cream or top milk to give a good consistency.

Serves 4.

# Felafel

Here is a favourite Middle-Eastern snack. Serve them with sauce and green salad or in wholemeal rolls, or – better still – in pita bread. Most recipes for felafel use minced soaked chick peas, without egg. This way is quicker if you have ground, toasted chick peas on hand, but it needs egg to bind the mixture.

8 oz (225g) ground, toasted chick peas (see p.20)
2 cloves garlic
Sea-salt to taste
3 tablespoonsful finely chopped parsley
2 tablespoonsful finely chopped green pepper
1½ teaspoonsful ground coriander, or to taste
1 teaspoonful cumin seed
1 medium onion
1 teaspoonful baking powder
1 oz (25g) butter, softened
1 large egg
Vegetable oil for frying
Chilli tomato sauce (see p.32)

Weigh out the ground chick peas and put them in a mixing bowl. Peel the garlic and crush well with a little salt. Add to the bowl with the parsley, chopped pepper, coriander and cumin. Peel the onion and grate into the bowl. Mix in the baking powder, beat in the butter and egg and mix thoroughly. Add more salt if needed. Form the mixture into small patties about ¾ inch (2cm) thick and fry in shallow oil, turning once, until crisp and brown. Serve with chilli tomato sauce.

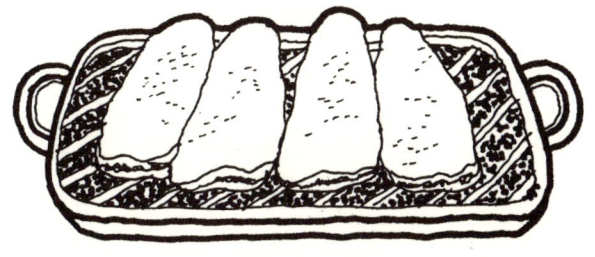

# Hummus

This is usually made in the liquidizer using cooked chick peas, but I prefer the following method – it is quicker and there is less clearing up. It is a great favourite – never leave a bowl of hummus where the 'nibblers' in the family can find it!

**4 oz (100g) ground, toasted chick peas (see p.20)**
**5 tablespoonsful water**
**2 cloves garlic**
**5 tablespoonsful lemon juice**
**3 tablespoonsful olive oil**
**2 tablespoonsful *tahini* (sesame seed paste)**
**Sea-salt**
**Olive oil and paprika to garnish**

Cook the ground chick peas in the water for a few minutes, stirring well with a wooden spoon, until they form a thick paste. Add a little more water if necessary. Turn into a bowl and cool.

Peel the garlic and crush with salt. Add garlic, lemon juice, olive oil and *tahini* to the chick pea paste and beat well together with a fork. If the mixture is too thick add a little more water. It should be thick but creamy.

Taste and add more salt, lemon juice or garlic if necessary. Turn into a small bowl. Spoon olive oil lightly over the surface and sprinkle with paprika to give colour. Serve with crusty wholemeal rolls, French bread or pita bread.

Serves 4.

# Lentil Pâté

Good with crispbreads or in sandwiches. If you like more garlic, fry a cut clove with the mushrooms before mixing with the lentils.

**2 eggs**
**2 oz (50g) lentils, any type, finely ground (see p.19)**
**6 tablespoonsful water**
**1 oz (25g) walnuts, finely milled**
**1 tablespoonful grated onion**
**4 oz (100g) mushrooms**
**2 oz (50g) butter**
**1 large clove garlic**
**½ lemon**
**1 tablespoonful chopped parsley**
**Sea-salt**
**Freshly-ground black pepper**

Hard-boil the eggs. Mix the ground lentils with half the water in a small, strong saucepan. Cook, stirring constantly, over low heat for about ten minutes, adding more water as needed, until the lentils cook to a thick paste. Turn out into a basin to cool and mix in the walnuts and grated onion.

Wash and drain the mushrooms and chop finely. Cook in half the butter in a frying pan over fairly high heat, stirring constantly, until beginning to soften. Cool.

Shell and chop the eggs. Mix chopped mushrooms and eggs with the lentil mixture and remaining butter. Rub a small serving dish well with a cut clove of garlic.

Season the *pâté* with salt, pepper, lemon juice and parsley. Grate in about two teaspoonsful of lemon rind. Spoon into the serving dish, cover and refrigerate until needed.

# Stir-fried Bean Sprouts with Almonds

Bean sprouts are deliciously crunchy but they need a lot of extra flavouring – fresh ginger is particularly good.

**12 oz (350g) bean sprouts**
**1 medium onion**
**2 cloves garlic**
**3 tablespoonsful grated fresh ginger root**
**Vegetable oil for frying**
**2-3 oz (50-75g) almonds**
**1 oz (25g) butter**
**1 tablespoonful soya sauce, or to taste**
**2 tablespoonsful sherry**
**2 teaspoonsful soft, brown sugar**
**Sea-salt**
**Freshly-ground black pepper**
**2 tablespoonsful chopped parsley**

Wash the bean sprouts well, discarding any which have discoloured, drain and dry on a tea towel. Peel and chop the onion and garlic and fry with the grated ginger in a little hot oil in a large frying pan until soft and beginning to brown.

Meanwhile, blanch and split the almonds and fry them in butter in a separate pan until golden brown. Drain and reserve.

Add beansprouts, soya sauce, sherry and sugar to the onion and stir-fry briskly for about four minutes or until heated through. Add sea-salt if required, remembering that the soya sauce is already salty, and pepper to taste. Fold in the almonds. Turn into a heated serving dish and sprinkle with parsley.

Serves 4.

*Variations*

*Mushrooms.* Fry 2-3 oz (50-75g) finely sliced mushrooms with the onion and garlic.

*Celery.* Add 2 sticks celery, finely sliced.

*Omelette strips.* For a more substantial dish, make 4 eggs into 3-4 thin, flat omelettes, cut into strips and arrange on top of the bean sprouts.

# Pipérade

Any beans may be used – they should be soft but not overcooked, or they may break up. Red kidney beans or butter beans are suitable. This is an adaptation of a Basque dish – a rather more adventurous form of scrambled eggs. If you like garlic, try replacing the fried bread triangles with fingers of bread spread with garlic butter and then toasted.

1 small onion
1 clove garlic
1 oz (25g) butter
1 medium green or red pepper
4 ripe tomatoes
4 oz (100g) cooked beans
2-3 slices wholemeal bread
Vegetable oil and butter for frying
4 eggs
2 tablespoonsful milk
Sea-salt
Freshly-ground black pepper

Peel and chop the onion and garlic and cook gently in the butter in a non-stick saucepan until beginning to soften and colour. Cut the pepper into thin strips, removing seeds and membrane, add to the pan and cook for five minutes. Peel and chop the tomatoes, add to the pan with the beans and allow to cook gently for a further four to five minutes. Cut the bread into triangles and fry until crisp in a mixture of oil and butter. Drain well and keep hot.

Beat up the eggs with milk, season well and pour into the pan with the vegetables. Stir with a wooden spoon until the eggs are just set. Turn out onto a hot serving dish and serve with the fried bread.

Serves 2.

# Lentil Stew with Dumplings

A complete meal, swift and nutritious, using the pressure cooker. Just add a green vegetable or a side salad.

**1 large onion**
**2 cloves garlic**
**2 tablespoonsful vegetable oil**
**2 oz (50g) butter**
**12 oz (350g) potatoes**
**2 medium carrots**
**2 large sticks celery**
**2 pts (1 litre) vegetable stock (see p.28)**
**8 oz (225g) continental lentils**
**Grated rind of 1 large orange**
**2 teaspoonsful chopped sage** *or*
**1 teaspoonful dried sage**
**Sea-salt**
**Freshly-ground black pepper**
**2 tablespoonsful chopped parsley**

*For the Dumplings*
**6 oz (175g) wholemeal flour**
**3 teaspoonsful baking powder**
**Sea-salt**
**Freshly-ground black pepper**
**1½ oz (40g) butter**
**1 medium egg**
**3 tablespoonsful milk (approx)**

Peel and chop onion and garlic and fry gently in the butter and oil in the pressure cooker until beginning to soften. Peel potatoes and cut into fairly small, even-sized pieces. Scrape and slice carrots, wash and roughly chop celery. Add vegetables to the cooker and continue frying for a few minutes over moderate heat, stirring with a wooden spoon. Add the stock. Wash lentils well, drain and add to the pan with the orange rind, sage, salt and pepper. Close cooker, bring to pressure and cook for 20 minutes.

Meanwhile, make the dumplings. Mix flour, baking

powder, salt and pepper. Rub in the butter. Beat the
eggs with two tablespoonsful milk and mix quickly with
the flour to make a stiff dough, adding a little more milk
if needed. Reduce pressure quickly and check that lentils
are cooked.

Roll the dough into very small dumplings and arrange
them on top of the stew. Replace the lid to cover the pan
but do not fasten down. If preferred, cover with foil or
with a plate. Cook at a gentle boil for ten minutes, or
until dumplings are firm. Sprinkle with chopped parsley
before serving.

Serves 4-6.

# Chick Pea Patties

Quickly made for lunch or supper – serve with watercress and a tomato and cucumber salad.

**6 oz (175g) ground, toasted chick peas (see p.20)**
**½ pt (275ml) water**
**1 medium onion**
**2 oz (50g) shelled walnuts**
**2 oz (50g) rolled oats**
**2 teaspoonsful dried marjoram**
**2 teaspoonsful chopped parsley**
**1 teaspoonful sea-salt**
**Vegetable oil**

Mix the ground chick peas with the water in a strong pan and cook over low heat, stirring well, for about five minutes to make a thick paste. Turn into a bowl to cool. Peel and chop onion, peel and crush garlic. Mill walnuts or chop finely. Mix all ingredients well, then form into eight patties.

The mixture should be moist enough to shape with the hands, but if too dry add a little oil. Flatten the patties and fry over moderate heat in a lightly oiled pan until brown, turning once to cook second side.

Serves 2-3.

CLIVE BIRCH

# 4
# SALADS, VEGETABLES AND JUST BEANS

Pulses blend beautifully with fruit and vegetable dishes and, of course, help to boost their nutritional content. Try experimenting with small quantities of several different salads set out on a large platter – it gives variety to meals and helps you to build up a collection of favourite bean recipes.

I have also included some standbys which are just beans, such as Baked Beans and Beans au Gratin. Use them as an extra vegetable, or make them the basis of a light meal with green vegetables or salads.

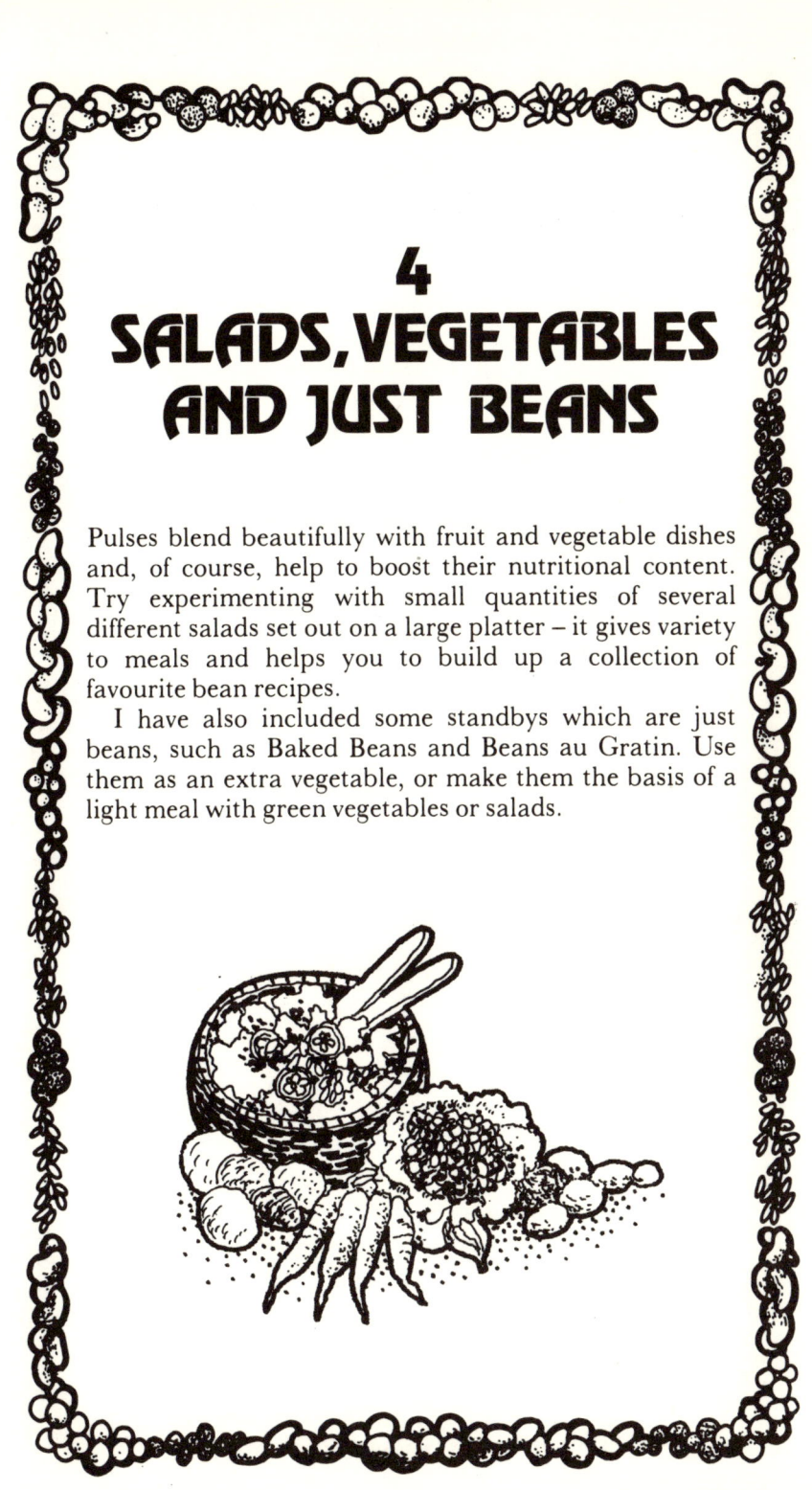

# Chick Pea Salad

Use either of these as part of a mixed salad meal. Cooked chick peas from the freezer are very suitable as most of the skins may be rubbed off as they thaw.

*With Walnuts and Apple*
**4 oz (100g) walnuts**
**2 dessert apples**
**8 oz (225g) cooked chick peas**
**2 tablespoonsful chopped parsley**
**Garlic French dressing (see p.34)**
**1 medium onion**

Chop the walnuts roughly, peel and chop the apples. Put walnuts, apples and chick peas into a shallow bowl, mix with the chopped parsley and toss in just enough garlic French dressing to coat. Peel the onion, slice thinly and arrange the rings on top of the salad.

*With Pineapple*
**6 oz (175g) canned pineapple, drained weight**
**5 tablespoonsful juice from the pineapple**
**5 tablespoonsful lemon juice**
**10 tablespoonsful corn oil**
**2 teaspoonsful grated, fresh ginger root**
**Sea-salt**
**Freshly-ground black pepper**
**Pinch light, soft, brown sugar**
**8 oz (225g) cooked chick peas**

Chop the pineapple into small pieces. Mix together the pineapple juice, lemon juice and corn oil, add the grated ginger root and season to taste with salt, pepper and sugar. Put the pineapple and chick peas in a small bowl, pour the dressing over and leave to stand for half an hour, stirring occasionally, so that the flavours may blend well.

Serves 3-4.

# Avocado and Soya Bean Salad

A solitary avocado will go round if you mix it with beans and use it as part of the salad plate. Avocados, by the way, should be almost black when you use them – far riper than we normally see them in the shops.

**1 ripe avocado**
**1 tablespoonful lemon juice**
**8 oz (225g) cooked soya beans**
**4 oz (100g) raisins**
**2 dessert apples**
**2 tablespoonsful French dressing (see p.34)**
**2-3 tablespoonsful mayonnaise (see p.35)**
**Watercress**

Halve the avocado, remove stone, scoop flesh out into a bowl and chop roughly. Toss in lemon juice. Add the soya beans and raisins. Peel, core and chop the apples and add to the bowl with the French dressing. Mix well. Fold in the mayonnaise and garnish with watercress.
  Serves 3-4.

# Carrot, Bean and Cress Salad

Cress and watercress are often far better buys in the winter than hot-house lettuce, which often has a sad, damp flannel taste. Watercress must be added to dressings at the very last moment before serving, as it wilts almost instantly.

**3 medium carrots**
**4 oz (100g) cooked beans, any type**
**1 dessert apple**
**1 small bunch watercress or punnet of cress**
**2 tablespoonsful chopped walnuts**
**2 oz (50g) raisins**
**French dressing (see p.34)**

Scrape the carrots and grate coarsely or shred in a vegetable mill. Peel, core and chop the apple. Toss together in enough French dressing to moisten well. Wash, drain and dry the watercress or cress and add to the salad with the nuts, raisins and beans. Add a little more dressing and serve at once.

Serves 4.

# Red Bean and Cheese Salad

A good lunch time salad, particularly with crusty rolls and a glass of wine.

**1 lb (450g) cooked red kidney beans**
**4 medium potatoes**
**French dressing (see p.34)**
**2 sticks celery**
**2 dessert apples**
**Grated rind and juice of ½ lemon**
**2-3 oz (50-75g) blue cheese**

Drain beans well. Scrub potatoes, cut into even-sized pieces and cook in boiling, salted water until just tender. Drain and skin. Slice potatoes and toss in dressing while still warm. Scrub and chop celery. Peel, core and chop the apples. Mix beans, potatoes, celery and apple and add just enough dressing to moisten well. Add lemon juice to taste and turn salad into a serving dish. Sprinkle with a little grated lemon rind and top with crumbled cheese.

*Variation*
*Red kidney bean and egg.* Make as above, but garnish with sliced hard-boiled eggs (1 per person) instead of cheese and top with onion rings and chopped parsley.
Serves 4-6.

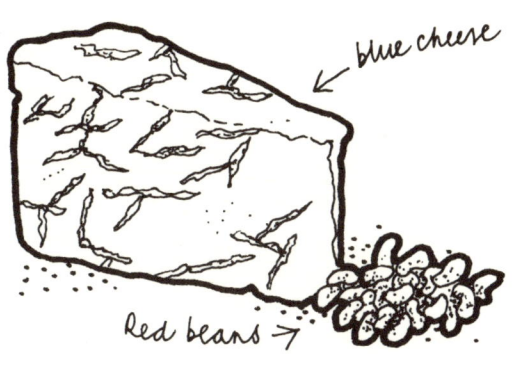

blue cheese

Red beans →

# Winter Salad

Both cabbage and beans go well with a tangy yogurt dressing. This is a good basis for a winter salad meal – add a handful of nuts, or any chopped fresh fruit as available.

**8 oz (225g) firm white cabbage**
**1 medium onion**
**2 dessert apples**
**8 oz (225g) cooked beans, any type**
**Yogurt dressing (see p.34)**

Trim any discoloured leaves from the cabbage, cut in chunks and wash well. Drain thoroughly and pat dry on a tea towel. Peel the onion and slice thinly. Peel and chop the apples, keeping one or two wedges unpeeled for garnish. Shred the cabbage finely into a salad bowl, mix with the chopped apple and beans and toss in yogurt dressing. Garnish with thin slices of unpeeled apple.
  Serves 4-6.

# Lemon Cream Bean Salad

Use black-eyed or borlotti beans, or mix different types of cooked beans already on hand.

**8 oz (225g) cooked beans**
**2 tomatoes**
**1 medium onion**
**½ cucumber**
**2 tablespoonsful chopped parsley**
**Lemon cream dressing (see p.35)**

Make sure that the beans are well drained. Slice the tomatoes, peel and thinly slice the onion and cucumber. Turn beans, tomatoes, onion and parsley into a bowl and mix well with just enough lemon cream dressing to coat.
  Serves 4.

# Bean and Potato Salad

Goes well with cold egg or cheese dishes. Team it with a bowl of crisp lettuce or watercress.

**8 oz (225g) potatoes
8 oz (225g) cooked beans, any type
3 tablespoonsful French dressing (see p.34)
2 tablespoonsful single cream
1 tablespoonful capers
1 medium onion
2 tablespoonsful chopped parsley**

Scrub potatoes and cook in boiling, salted water until just tender. Cool slightly, then peel and slice thickly while still warm. Mix with the beans and toss in French dressing. Stir the cream in gently so that the potatoes do not break up. Stir in the capers and half the parsley. Garnish with onion rings and the remaining parsley.
  Serves 4.

# Greek Bean Salad

Fennel seeds give a delicious aniseed flavour. Serve as part of a mixed salad meal, or top with sliced tomatoes and wedges of hard-boiled egg for a light lunch dish.

**6 oz (175g) haricot beans
3 bay leaves
3-4 strips lemon peel
2 teaspoonsful fennel seeds
4 tablespoonsful lemon juice
3 tablespoonsful olive oil
Sea-salt
Freshly-ground black pepper
1 large clove garlic
2 tablespoonsful chopped parsley**

Soak beans overnight. Drain, rinse and cook in fresh water with lemon peel, bay leaves and 1 teaspoonful fennel seeds. Make a dressing with the lemon juice, oil and remaining fennel seeds, crushed or ground. Season with salt and pepper. Rub a serving dish well with the cut clove of garlic.

When the beans are cooked, drain and mix with the dressing while still hot. When cool, stir in the chopped parsley and adjust seasoning, adding more oil or lemon juice if required.

Serves 3-4.

# Curried Butter Bean Salad

Use as part of a mixed salad meal, or with hard-boiled eggs and cucumber. Butter beans go particularly well with curry flavouring and mayonnaise.

**8 oz (225g) cooked butter beans**
**4 tablespoonsful mayonnaise**
**½ teaspoonful curry powder, or to taste**
**2 teaspoonsful desiccated coconut**
**2 teaspoonsful mango chutney**
**Sea-salt to taste**
**Squeeze of lemon juice**

Make sure that the beans are well drained. Mix mayonnaise with curry powder, coconut and chutney. Mix beans in lightly, being careful not to break them up, and season with salt and lemon juice.
    Serves 2-3.

# Leek, Bean and Olive Salad

Young leeks make such a delicious salad that I like to serve it separately as a first course. Do not be tempted to overcook them.

**6-8 young leeks**
**8 oz (225g) cooked butter beans or haricot beans**
**French dressing (see p.34)**
**Lemon juice**
**A few black olives**

Trim the leeks, removing any damaged leaves, but retaining most of the green. Cut them down the centre and wash very thoroughly under running cold water. Cook the leeks in boiling salted water for a few minutes only. Do not let them soften completely. Drain well (the cooking water may be used for soups) and gently press out as much liquid as possible. Toss the leeks in French dressing while still warm, and arrange on a shallow dish. Mix the beans with a little more dressing and spoon over the leeks. Add lemon juice to taste and garnish with olives.
    Serves 4.

# Bean Sprout and Cucumber Salad

Crunchy bean sprouts taste even crunchier if you add wholemeal *croûtons* to the salad. This is good as a starter.

**4 oz (100g) bean sprouts**
**½ cucumber**
**1 small onion**
**2 oz (50g) button mushrooms**
**French dressing (see p.34)**
**Lemon juice**
**Sea-salt**
**3 slices dry wholemeal bread**
**Vegetable oil for frying**

Rinse bean sprouts well and drain thoroughly. Peel and chop the cucumber. Peel the onion and slice thinly. Wash, drain and dry the mushrooms, slice and mix with the bean sprouts and vegetables. Toss well in just enough French dressing to coat and add extra lemon juice to taste with a pinch of sea-salt if needed.

Cut the bread into small cubes and fry in hot oil until crisp and brown. Drain well and mix lightly into the salad just before serving.

Serves 2-3.

# Oriental Bean Sprout Salad

This looks particularly attractive if you can find a bright red pepper to mix with the bean sprouts. Use as part of a mixed salad meal.

**4 oz (100g) bean sprouts**
**1 medium red or green pepper**
**1 dessert apple**
**1 tablespoonful honey**
**1 tablespoonful lemon juice**
**2 tablespoonsful wine or cider vinegar**
**1 teaspoonful soya sauce, or to taste**

Pick over bean sprouts, wash well and dry. De-seed and slice the pepper; peel, core and chop the apple. Mix the honey, lemon juice, vinegar and soya sauce together in a salad bowl. Add bean sprouts, pepper and apple and toss well together. Taste and sprinkle in a little more soya sauce if needed.

Serves 2-3.

# Bean Sprout and Orange Salad

A tangy, crunchy salad. Combine it with bland tastes such as egg or potato when making up a salad meal.

**12 oz (350g) bean sprouts**
**French dressing (see p.34)**
**8 oz (225g) cucumber**
**2 large oranges**
**Sea-salt**
**1 tablespoonful lemon juice**
**1-2 teaspoonsful grated lemon rind**
**1-2 teaspoonsful grated fresh ginger**
**12 oz (350g) cottage cheese**
**Twists of orange peel to garnish**

Pick over bean sprouts and discard any which have discoloured. Wash bean sprouts well, drain and dry on tea towels. Toss in French dressing. Peel and slice cucumber, peel and section the oranges and mix lightly with the bean sprouts. Add lemon juice, grated lemon rind and ginger to taste. Arrange on a serving dish, top with cottage cheese and garnish with orange peel twists.
    Serves 4.

# Marinated Beans and Mushrooms

Serve with crusty bread, either as a first course or as part of a salad meal.

**12 oz (350g) button mushrooms**
**Juice of 1 lemon**
**1 clove garlic**
**1 onion**
**½ pt (275ml) wine or cider vinegar**
**Bunch of herbs (parsley, thyme, bay leaf, savory)** *or*
**sachet dried** *bouquet garni*
**Sea-salt**
**Freshly-ground black pepper**
**½ pt (275ml) corn oil**
**1 tablespoonful tomato** *purée*
**8 oz (225g) cooked beans such as butter beans, black,**
**red kidney, pinto etc.**
**Light, soft, brown sugar**
**Chopped parsley**

Wash and drain the mushrooms. Cook for five minutes only in boiling, salted water with the lemon juice added. Drain well. Peel the onion and cut in large sections, cutting from top to bottom. Peel and split the garlic. Bring the vinegar to the boil in a small pan and simmer for five minutes with the onion, garlic, the herbs tied with cotton and a pinch of salt and pepper.

Remove the garlic and leave the vinegar to cool. When it is quite cold, mix with the oil and tomato *purée*. Add a little sugar if the marinade is too sharp. Pour it over the mushrooms and beans in a deep bowl. Leave for three to four hours in a cool place, turning occasionally. Remove the bunch of herbs and the onion and sprinkle with parsley before serving.

Serves 4-6.

# Ratatouille with Beans

Make delicious ratatouille at the end of the summer when tomatoes come down in price and there are plenty of marrows and fresh herbs. Add cooked pulses and it becomes a meal on its own. Serve hot to accompany other dishes, or cold with crusty bread for a light lunch..

**1 lb (450g) tomatoes**
**1 lb (450g) courgettes or marrow**
**1 medium aubergine**
**8 oz (225g) mushrooms**
**1 large onion**
**1 green or red pepper**
**2 cloves garlic, or to taste**
**3-4 tablespoonsful olive oil**
**1 tablespoonful chopped, fresh herbs**
**Sea-salt**
**Freshly-ground black pepper**
**8-12 oz (225-275g) cooked beans, any type**

Skin and roughly chop the tomatoes and wash and slice courgettes and aubergine, without peeling. If using a large marrow, peel it, remove the seeds, then cut marrow into slices. Wash and chop the mushrooms. Wash and de-seed the pepper and cut into strips. Peel and chop onion and garlic.

Heat the oil in a large, shallow pan with a lid, or use a frying pan and cover with foil or a large saucepan lid. Cook the mushrooms, onion, garlic and pepper together gently for about five minutes. Then add all remaining ingredients except the beans. Season well and cook, stirring occasionally with a wooden spoon, until the tomato is soft. Cover the pan, set it on a wire mesh or asbestos mat and cook very gently for about one hour. The vegetables should be well blended and soft.

Add the beans and cook, uncovered, stirring, until they are heated through. Raise the heat, if necessary, to drive off any excess moisture. Adjust the seasoning. Serve hot or cold.

Serves 4-6.

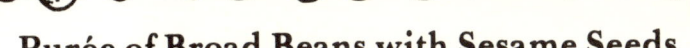

# Purée of Broad Beans with Sesame Seeds

Dried broad beans have a good flavour but tough skins. They also take a long time to cook. It is best to soak them overnight, then cook in the pressure cooker and make into a *purée*. Toasted sesame seeds team well with them. Use to accompany any savoury dish.

**8 oz (225g) dried broad beans**
**1 oz (25g) butter**
**Sea-salt**
**Freshly-ground black pepper**
**4 tablespoonsful single cream or top milk**
**2 tablespoonsful sesame seeds**
**2-3 teaspoonsful chopped parsley**

Soak beans overnight, rinse and cook, preferably in a pressure cooker, until quite soft but not breaking up. While beans are cooking, spread the sesame seeds on the grill pan and toast, shaking frequently, until a good, golden brown.

Drain the beans, reserving the cooking water. Put the beans in the liquidizer goblet with just enough cooking water to make the machine run smoothly. Reduce to a *purée*.

Melt the butter in a saucepan, then rub the beans through a coarse sieve into the pan. Season with salt and pepper. Stir in the cream and reheat gently but do not boil. Turn the *purée* into a heated serving dish and top with the sesame seeds and a sprinkling of chopped parsley.

Serves 3-4.

# Mexican Fried Beans

If you are in a hurry, these beans may be cooked in one operation, but they are known in Mexico as *frijoles refritos* and the second frying does improve the flavour.

**1 lb (450g) cooked red kidney beans**
**Vegetable oil**
**1 large onion**
**2-3 teaspoonsful tomato** *purée*
**Chilli sauce to taste**

Make sure that the beans are well drained. Fry them in a little oil over moderate heat, mashing them down with a fork during cooking. When the beans are hot and beginning to become crisp, add about a teacupful of water and continue cooking over low heat until the mixture becomes dry again. Cool the beans and refrigerate overnight or until required. To serve, peel and chop the onion and fry in 1 tablespoonful oil until soft. Add the beans, tomato *purée* and a dash of chilli sauce. Cook, stirring well, until heated through.

# Baked Beans

Baked beans need long cooking to soften and to absorb seasoning flavours, so make when the oven is being used at least part of the time for other dishes. Left over beans may be kept for another day and gently reheated in the saucepan.

**8 oz (225g) haricot beans**
**1 large onion**
**1 large clove garlic**
**1 tablespoonful vegetable oil**
**14 oz (400g) can tomatoes**
**1 tablespoonful black treacle**
**1 tablespoonful soft, brown sugar**
**½ teaspoonful chilli sauce**
**½ teaspoonful dry mustard**
**Sea-salt to taste**

Soak beans overnight in plenty of water. Drain, rinse and drain again. Peel and chop onion. Peel and crush garlic. Fry onion and garlic in the oil until soft and beginning to brown. Add the drained beans, the tomatoes, treacle, sugar, chilli sauce and mustard. Bring to the boil and turn into an ovenproof dish with a tightly fitting lid.

Cook in a fairly slow oven, 325°F/170°C (Gas Mark 3) for six to eight hours. A little water may be added during cooking if necessary, but the sauce should be thick. Add salt during the last two or three hours of cooking.

Serves 4.

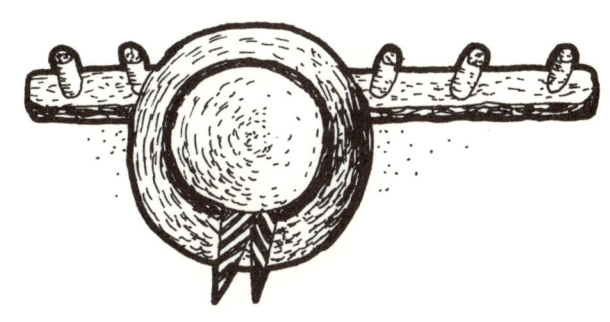

# Beans au Gratin

Any cooked beans may be used for this dish providing you add a really well flavoured tomato sauce. Serve with patties, croquettes or savouries, or in larger portions with salad for a light lunch.

**12 oz (350g) cooked haricot, butter or other beans**
**1 oz (25g) butter**
**Sea-salt to taste**
**Tomato sauce (see p.31)**
**2 oz (50g) grated cheese**
**2 oz (50g) wholemeal breadcrumbs**
**1 tablespoonful chopped parsley**

Toss the beans with the butter over low heat until warm. Add sea-salt to taste and transfer to a heatproof shallow dish. Heat the tomato sauce and spread over the beans. Mix the grated cheese, breadcrumbs and parsley and use as a topping, spreading evenly with a fork. Place the dish under a moderate grill until well browned and bubbling.
　Serves 3-4.

# Sweet and Sour Beans

Other beans may be substituted, but this recipe makes the most of the good, mealy texture of butter beans.

**1 medium onion**
**1 clove garlic**
**1 tablespoonful vegetable oil**
**1 tablespoonful wine or cider vinegar**
**1 tablespoonful soft, brown sugar**
**1 dessert apple**
**12 oz (350g) cooked butter beans**
**Sea-salt to taste**
**2 teaspoonsful chopped parsley**

Peel onion and slice thinly. Peel and crush garlic. Fry together in the oil over moderate heat until soft and beginning to brown. Add the vinegar and sugar and mix well. Remove from the heat. Peel the apple and grate directly into the pan. Return pan to the cooker, add the beans and stir all together over low heat until beans are hot through. Season with sea-salt. Turn into a heated serving dish and sprinkle with chopped parsley.

Serves 3-4.

# 5
# MAIN DISHES

The best dishes using pulses make a round-up of world cuisine – so many countries have discovered down the ages that tasty and economical meals may be based on peas, beans and lentils. I have collected ideas from as far afield as India, China, Mexico and Italy, plus a more homely Shepherd's Pie and a warming stew with dumplings.

## Khicharhi

The origins of 'kedgeree' lie in this Indian dish of rice and *moong dhal* (yellow lentils) with lots of spices. Cucumber salad goes well with it, but chunks of really ripe melon are particularly good.

2 oz (50g) long-grain, unpolished rice
1 tablespoonful chopped coriander leaves *or*
1 teaspoonful coriander seeds
½ inch (1cm) piece of fresh ginger root, peeled
2 cloves garlic, peeled
¼ teaspoonful chilli powder
½ teaspoonful turmeric
½ teaspoonful garam masala
1 large onion
1 tablespoonful vegetable oil
4 oz (100g) potato
4 oz (100g) yellow lentils, washed and drained
¼ teaspoonful cumin seeds
2 cardamom pods
1-inch (2.5cm) piece cinnamon bark
2 tomatoes
Sea-salt
Lemon juice

Cook the rice in boiling salted water until just tender. Drain well and reserve. Crush the coriander, ginger, garlic, chilli powder, turmeric and garam masala in a mortar to make a paste. Peel and chop the onion and fry in the oil until beginning to soften. Add the paste and stir together over moderate heat for a few minutes.

Peel and chop the potatoes and add to the pan with the lentils, rice, cumin seed, cardamom and cinnamon. Add the tomatoes cut in pieces and salt to taste. Add water to cover, bring to the boil and simmer gently for about 30 minutes or until lentils and potatoes are soft. Add a little more water during cooking if necessary, but the mixture should not be too wet. Remove cinnamon before serving.

Serves 2-3.

# Two Bean and Dumpling Stew

Serve with crusty bread for a warming winter supper.

*For the Stew*
**4 oz (100g) flageolets and 4 oz (100g) black eyed
beans – dry weight – soaked, cooked and drained
1 lb (450g) mixed root vegetables, peeled weight
1 medium onion
4 oz (100g) mushrooms
14 oz (400g) can tomatoes
3 tablespoonsful vegetable oil
2 pts (1 litre) vegetable stock (see p.28)
2 tablespoonsful tomato *purée*
Grated rind of 1 lemon
Sea-salt
Freshly-ground black pepper
2 tablespoonsful natural yogurt
2 tablespoonsful chopped parsley
2-3 tablespoonsful grated cheese**

*For the Dumplings*
**6 oz (175g) 81 per cent plain flour
½ teaspoonful sea-salt
1 teaspoonful baking powder
3 oz (75g) margarine
½ teaspoonful dried basil or tarragon**

Make the dumplings. Sift together the flour, salt and baking powder. Rub in margarine and add the dried herbs. Mix to a firm dough with a little water. Form into eight dumplings. Cut the peeled and trimmed vegetables into small dice. Peel and chop the onion. Slice mushrooms. Drain and chop tomatoes, reserving the juice. Heat the oil in a frying pan and fry vegetables gently, stirring constantly, for three to four minutes. Set aside.

Bring the stock to the boil in a large saucepan. Put in the dumplings and boil, covered, for three minutes. Add the fried vegetables, the chopped tomatoes and reserved juice, tomato *purée* and grated lemon rind. Mix together gently and simmer, covered, for 15 minutes. Add cooked beans and simmer for a further five minutes or until beans are heated through. Remove from heat, check seasoning and stir in yogurt. Serve sprinkled with the chopped parsley and grated cheese.

Serves 4.

# Split Pea Shepherd's Pie

A good standby for the winter months when turnips, carrots and swedes are at their best. Serve with a watercress or cabbage salad or a cooked green vegetable.

8 oz (225g) split peas
1 pt (575ml) vegetable stock (see p.28)
1 medium onion
1 clove garlic
2 carrots
2 sticks celery
1 small green pepper
2 tablespoonful vegetable oil
2 oz (50g) mushrooms
2-3 tablespoonful tomato juice and dash of chilli sauce *or*
2 tablespoonful tomato chilli sauce (see p.32)
½ teaspoonful dried thyme
½ teaspoonful ground mace
Sea-salt
Freshly-ground black pepper
2 large tomatoes

*For the Topping*
1½ lb (675g) potatoes
2 oz (50g) butter
3 tablespoonful single cream or top milk
2 teaspoonful dried basil
3 oz (75g) grated cheese
Sea-salt
Freshly-ground black pepper

Wash and drain split peas and cook, covered, in the stock until the peas are tender and the stock is absorbed (about one hour). Meanwhile, prepare the vegetables. Peel and chop the onion and garlic. Scrub the carrots and celery then cut into thin slices. De-seed and chop the pepper. Fry together in the vegetable oil for about 15 minutes or until carrot begins to soften. Wash and slice mushrooms and add to the pan towards the end of cooking. Mix in the cooked split peas, the tomato juice or chilli tomato sauce and the herbs and seasonings. Turn into a large pie dish. Slice the tomatoes and arrange on top.

Peel potatoes and cook in boiling salted water, or scrub and cook as they are, removing the skins before mashing. Heat the butter and cream together in a small pan. Mash potatoes, adding cream and butter, basil, grated cheese, salt and pepper. Beat well with a wooden spoon. Spread over the split pea mixture and bake at 375°F/190°C (Gas Mark 5) for 20-25 minutes or until heated through and lightly browned.

Serves 4.

## Risotto with Beans

A super 'one dish' light meal. The beans add to the protein content and it looks very appetizing with plenty of chopped parsley and a green side salad.

6 oz (175g) unpolished long-grain, rice
1 large onion
2 cloves garlic
2 tablespoonsful vegetable oil
1 oz (25g) butter
Sea-salt
Freshly-ground black pepper
1 pt (575ml) vegetable stock (see p.28)
8 oz (225g) cooked pinto beans
4 oz (100g) mushrooms
Butter
4 oz (100g) grated cheese
Chopped parsley

Pick over rice. If it needs washing, it must be thoroughly dried before use. Peel and chop onion and garlic and fry together in a strong saucepan in a mixture of oil and butter over moderate heat until beginning to soften. Add the rice and fry, stirring constantly, until the rice deepens slightly in colour and is well coated with butter. Add salt and pepper and about two-thirds of the stock. Bring to the boil, then cover the pan and set it on a wire or asbestos mat over very low heat.

After about 20 minutes, or when the rice begins to soften, slice the mushrooms, soften in a little butter and add to the pan with the beans and more stock if needed. When the rice is completely cooked and all liquid absorbed, stir in the chopped parsley and serve the risotto with grated cheese.

Serves 4.

# Pastichio

A combination of pulses and pasta sounds rather solid – pastichio is in fact a pleasantly light and flavoursome dish. Serve with watercress and a selection of salads.

6 oz (175g) continental lentils
1 large onion
1 clove garlic
1¾ lb (800g) can tomatoes
2 tablespoonsful vegetable oil
1 tablespoonful tomato *purée*
1 teaspoonful dried oregano
1 teaspoonful cinnamon
Pinch ground cloves
Pinch cayenne
1 bay leaf
1 teaspoonful soft, brown sugar
Sea-salt to taste
Freshly-ground black pepper
6 oz (175g) wholemeal noodles
¾ pt (425ml) white sauce (see p.29)
4 oz (100g) grated cheese
2 egg yolks

Cook lentils and drain. Peel and chop onion, peel and crush garlic. Drain tomatoes, reserving the liquid, and chop. Fry onion and garlic gently in the oil for a few minutes, then add the chopped tomatoes and juice, the tomato *purée*, herbs, spices and sugar. Cook gently, uncovered, for about 30 minutes or until the mixture has thickened. Mix with the cooked lentils and season well with salt and pepper.

Cook the noodles in plenty of boiling salted water and drain. Make the white sauce. Add the grated cheese, stirring well over low heat. Remove from the heat and stir in egg yolks.

Butter a large, shallow ovenproof dish. Make a layer of noodles and cover with the lentil mixture. Spoon the cheese sauce over the top and bake at 350°F/180°C (Gas Mark 4) for 40-50 minutes until nicely browned.

Serves 6.

# Butter Bean and Mixed Vegetable Pie

Stuffed tomatoes go well with this pie and may be cooked in the oven at the same time.

**4 oz (100g) butter beans**
**2 medium onions**
**8 oz (225g) potatoes**
**1 leek**
**6 oz (175g) white cabbage**
**4 oz (100g) mushrooms**
**3 tablespoonsful vegetable oil**
**1 teaspoonful dill seed**
**1 teaspoonful dried thyme**
**2 tablespoonsful tomato** *purée*
**½ pt (275ml) vegetable stock (see p.28)**
**1 tablespoonful wholemeal flour**
**Sea-salt**
**Freshly-ground black pepper**
**Flaky pastry made with 6 oz (175g) flour (see p.36)**

Soak and cook butter beans. Drain. Peel and slice onions then peel and slice potatoes. Trim, wash and chop leek. Shred cabbage, wash and slice mushrooms. Heat the oil in a medium-sized saucepan, add onions, potatoes and cabbage. Stir well, cover and cook gently for five minutes. Add leek, mushrooms and herbs. Mix well so that the vegetables are well coated with oil.

Cook, covered, over low heat for 15 minutes. Remove from the heat, add tomato *purée* and stock. Sprinkle in the flour and stir to mix.

Finally, add the cooked beans and season well with salt and pepper. Transfer to a 2 pt (1 litre) pie dish. When bean mixture is cool, cover with pastry, sealing the edges well. Brush with milk or egg to glaze if you wish. Bake for 15 minutes at 425°F/220°C (Gas Mark 7) for 15 minutes, then reduce heat to 375°F/190°C (Gas Mark 5) for a further 20 minutes.
Serves 4.

# Bean and Cottage Cheese Flan

Flans like this one are nice for buffet meals or for 'no fuss' weekend lunches in the garden. You could precede it with a chilled soup and serve a range of colourful salads.

**Shortcrust pastry made with 10 oz (275g) flour (see p.35)**
**1 lb (450g) cottage cheese**
**4 eggs**
**6 oz (175g) cooked beans, any type**
**2 oz (50g) mushrooms**
**1 small onion**
**1 oz (25g) butter**
**2 teaspoonsful chopped fresh tarragon** *or*
**1 teaspoonful dried tarragon**
**Sea-salt**
**Freshly-ground black pepper**
**4 tomatoes**
**2 oz (50g) grated cheese**
**Chopped parsley**

Make the pastry and line an 11-inch (28cm) flan tin. Turn the cottage cheese into a basin and break up with a fork. Beat in the eggs and mix well. Stir in the cooked beans. Wash the mushrooms and slice thinly. Peel and chop the onion and fry gently in the butter with the mushrooms until beginning to soften. Reserve a few of the best mushroom slices and mix the rest of the mushroom and onion mixture with the eggs, cheese and beans, together with the tarragon and a seasoning of salt and pepper. Spoon into the flan case.

Slice the tomatoes and arrange on top with the reserved mushroom slices. Sprinkle with grated cheese and bake at 400°F/200°C (Gas Mark 6) for 15 minutes. Reduce the heat to 325°F/170°C (Gas Mark 3) for about 20 minutes or until the filling is set. Garnish with chopped parsley.

Serves 4-6.

# Leek and Bean Tartlets

Leeks are a rather neglected vegetable, I feel. They are delicious mixed with beans in flans and savouries, and their delicate flavour appeals to many people who do not like too much onion.

**Shortcrust pastry made with 8 oz (225g) flour (see p.35)**
**2 medium leeks**
**½ pt (275ml) milk**
**2 oz (50g) margarine**
**2 oz (50g) 81 per cent plain flour**
**12 oz (350g) cooked beans**
**Sea-salt**
**Freshly-ground black pepper**
**1 oz (25g) almonds**
**3-4 oz (75-100g) grated cheese**
**2 tablespoonsful wholemeal breadcrumbs**

Roll out pastry and line four individual baking tins or foil pie plates. Prick the pastry well with a fork and bake blind at 400°F/200°C (Gas Mark 6) for about twelve minutes, or until set but not brown. Remove from the oven. Meanwhile, trim leeks, slice thickly and wash well. Cook in a little boiling salted water until just tender. Drain thoroughly, reserving the cooking water.

Measure ½ pt (275ml) cooking water and mix with the milk. Use to make a thick white sauce with the margarine and flour (see p.29). Stir in the cooked leeks and beans. Blanch, toast and chop the almonds and add to the mixture. Season well with salt and pepper. Divide between the pastry cases and sprinkle with a mixture of grated cheese and breadcrumbs. Place under a moderate grill until the cheese has melted and the crumbs are lightly browned.

Serves 4.

# Curried Pasties

Based on the Indian *samosas*, these little pasties make a good hot dish with rice and a salad, or a tasty addition to picnics or lunch boxes when cold.

**4 oz (100g) split red lentils**
**¾ pt (425ml) water**
**1 medium onion**
**½ oz (15g) fresh ginger root**
**2 dessert apples**
**2 tablespoonsful vegetable oil**
**1 teaspoonful turmeric**
**1 teaspoonful ground coriander**
**1 teaspoonful cumin**
**2 oz (50g) sultanas**
**Sea-salt to taste**
**Shortcrust or flaky pastry made with 12 oz (350g)**
**flour (see pp.36/38)**
**Vegetable oil for deep frying**

Grind lentils to a fine powder (see p.19). Mix with the water, bring to the boil and simmer gently until the water is absorbed. Meanwhile, peel and chop onion and ginger. Peel, core and chop apples. Fry the onion and ginger gently in the oil with the spices for about five minutes, stirring occasionally. Add chopped apple and sultanas, three tablespoonsful water and salt to taste.

Cook gently until onion and apples are soft. Add to lentils and cool. Roll out pastry and cut into circles about 3½ inches (9cm) diameter. Divide the mixture between half the circles, moisten edges, top with remaining circles, press down edges and seal well. Deep fry two at a time until well browned. Drain on kitchen paper.

Makes about 10.

# Summertime Pizza

Perhaps I should say late summer pizza, when there are lots of lovely ripe tomatoes. In the winter you can make a quick version (see p.52) using scone dough and a sauce made with canned tomatoes.

*For the Pizza Dough*
½ teaspoonful soft, brown sugar
3 tablespoonsful tepid water
½ oz (15g) dried baking yeast
8 oz (225g) wholemeal flour
1 teaspoonful sea-salt
2 eggs
2 oz (50g) butter

*For the Topping*
1½ lb (675g) ripe tomatoes
1 onion
1 clove garlic
1 tablespoonful vegetable oil
1 bay leaf
Sea-salt
Freshly-ground black pepper
Dash of sherry (optional)
8 oz (225g) cooked beans, any type
4 oz (100g) grated cheese
A few black olives
2-3 teaspoonsful fresh or dried herbs

Stir the sugar into the tepid water, add the yeast and leave in a warm place for about ten minutes to froth up. Sift the flour and salt into a warmed bowl, returning to the bowl any bran left in the sieve. The eggs and butter should be at room temperature. Beat the eggs into the yeast mixture. Add to the flour and mix well. Work in the butter. Cover the bowl with a tea towel or put it in a large plastic bag. Leave the dough to rise for about 45 minutes in a moderately warm place. It should double in bulk.

Meanwhile, make the topping. Skin and chop the tomatoes. Peel and chop the onion and garlic and fry gently in the oil until beginning to soften. Add tomatoes and bay leaf and season lightly. Cook over moderate heat until the tomatoes are soft, then turn up the heat and reduce to a thick *purée*, stirring well. Add the sherry and mix in the cooked beans. Remove bay leaf, adjust seasoning and turn the mixture into a basin to cool.

Put a large piece of foil on a baking sheet and flour it lightly. Place the pizza dough on it and pat it into a circle about 9 inches (23cm) across. Spread the bean and tomato mixture on it to within a half-inch (1cm) of the edges. Top with the grated cheese, decorate with olives and sprinkle with herbs. Leave to 'prove' in a warm place for 15 minutes, then bake at 400°F/200°C (Gas Mark 6) for about 20 minutes.

Serves 6-8.

# Creamy Sesame Croquettes

Delicious little croquettes are simple to prepare, particularly if you make the casing and filling ahead of time and refrigerate. Be sure to let them come back to room temperature before making up and frying the croquettes. Allow two for each person as part of a snack lunch, or three to four each for a main dish with salad or green vegetables.

4 oz (100g) continental lentils, ground (see p.19)
¼ pt (150ml) vegetable stock (see p.28)
1½ oz (40g) walnuts
2 tablespoonsful sesame seeds
2 oz (50g) wholemeal flour
½ teaspoonful baking powder
¼ teaspoonful sea-salt
1 egg
Filling (see following recipe)

Cook the ground lentils in the stock over moderate heat, stirring constantly with a wooden spoon, for about seven to eight minutes, or until they form a thick paste. Add a little more stock if necessary while cooking, but the mixture should be very stiff. Turn onto a plate to cool. Mill the walnuts finely. Toast the sesame seeds to a good golden brown, shaking the grill pan so that they do not burn.

Mix nuts and seeds in a bowl with the flour, baking powder and salt. Beat the egg and add to the bowl with the cold lentils. Mix together well with the fingers until the egg is absorbed. Form into a ball as for pastry, flour lightly, cover and refrigerate until needed.

To make the croquettes, roll the paste out about ¼-inch (½cm) thick. Flour the working surface well and sprinkle paste with flour, as it is soft to handle. Cut into eight rectangles. Divide filling between them, making sure that the croquettes will not be too full. With floured hands, roll them gently into sausage shapes and flatten slightly. Dust with flour and shallow fry in hot oil over moderate heat for about 5 minutes, turning carefully to brown both sides. Take care not to overheat the oil or the outside will burn before the filling is hot. The croquettes may be deep-fried if you prefer.

Makes 8.

# Egg and Mushroom Filling

1 egg, hard-boiled
3 oz (75g) mushrooms, washed and chopped
2 oz (50g) onion, peeled and chopped
½ oz (15g) butter
½ oz (15g) wholemeal breadcrumbs
2 tablespoonsful soured cream
1½ tablespoonsful chopped parsley
½ teaspoonful chopped thyme *or*
good pinch dried thyme
Sea-salt
Freshly-ground black pepper

Chop the hard-boiled egg. Make sure that the mushrooms are well drained. Fry the chopped onion in the butter over moderate heat until beginning to soften. Add chopped mushrooms, turn the heat up and fry briskly for a few minutes, stirring with a wooden spoon, until mushrooms are just soft. Turn into a basin to cool. Add the breadcrumbs and soured cream. (Use thick fresh cream or white sauce if soured cream is not available). Add herbs, salt and pepper. Mix well and taste. The mixture should be well seasoned. Cover and refrigerate until needed.

# Chick Pea and Tarragon Filling

6 oz (175g) cooked chick peas, well drained
¼ pt (150ml) thick white sauce (see p.29)
2 teaspoonsful dried tarragon
Sea-salt
Freshly-ground black pepper

Mix all ingredients, mashing the chick peas down lightly into the sauce. Cover and refrigerate until needed.

# Chilli Beans with Coconut

A delicious Mexican dish of beans with a creamy coconut sauce – make it just as spicy or fiery as you choose and let the vacuum jar do most of the cooking. Serve with plain rice and a cooling tomato and cucumber salad. If you are feeling extravagant, try chopped melon and cucumber with these hot dishes, tossed with a little French dressing.

**8 oz red kidney beans**
**1 medium onion**
**1 clove garlic**
**1 tablespoonful vegetable oil**
**1 teaspoonful chilli powder, or to taste**
**1 pt (575ml) vegetable stock (see p.28)**
**Sea-salt**
**1 oz (25g) creamed coconut**
**Dash Tabasco sauce (optional)**

Wash the beans and soak them overnight, or by the quick method (see p.12). Rinse and drain and soak again in fresh water while preparing the onion. Peel and chop the onion and garlic and fry in the vegetable oil over moderate heat until soft and beginning to brown. Add the chilli powder and fry for a few minutes longer, stirring well with a wooden spoon. Pour in the stock. Drain the beans and add to the pan. Bring to the boil and simmer for four to five minutes.

Heat the vacuum jar and spoon in the beans with enough stock to fill the jar and leave a small space under the stopper. Close and leave for at least six hours or overnight if more convenient. Pour the beans into a saucepan, bring back to the boil and simmer gently for about 20 minutes or until quite soft. Break up the creamed coconut with a fork and mix to a cream with a little of the liquid from the pan. Stir into the bean mixture and add sea-salt to taste. If creamed coconut is not available, desiccated coconut may be used instead, but the sauce will not be so smooth.

Serves 4.

## Stuffed Jacket Potatoes

Known in my family as 'skin potatoes', these old favourites become even more nutritious and tasty with the addition of beans or peas, herbs and cheese.

*With Beans*
**4 large baking potatoes**
**8 oz (225g) cooked small beans, e.g. adzuki, red kidney, haricot, etc.**
**3-4 oz (75-100g) cream cheese**
**2 teaspoonsful chopped rosemary**
**2 teaspoonsful chopped parsley**
**1 teaspoonful grated lemon rind**
**Sea-salt**
**Freshly-ground black pepper**
**Butter (optional)**

*With Chick Peas*
**4 large baking potatoes**
**2 oz (50g) ground toasted chick peas (see p.20)**
**3 tablespoonsful chopped parsley**
**2 oz (50g) butter**
**Sea-salt**
**Freshly-ground black pepper**
**Extra butter (optional)**

Scrub the potatoes well, score with a sharp knife to prevent bursting and bake in a moderate oven, 350°F/180°C (Gas Mark 4) until cooked – between one and two hours according to the size and type of potato. When the potatoes are soft, cut them in half and scoop the centres out carefully into a bowl, reserving the skins. Mash the potato in the bowl, add the beans or peas, cream cheese or butter and season with herbs, lemon rind, salt and pepper etc. Pack into the potato skins, mounding the filling. Reheat in the oven. If you wish to brown the tops, dot with extra butter and finish under the grill.
Serves 4.

# Lentil Cutlets

Make well ahead of time and keep in a cool place until it is time to prepare the meal. Serve with a selection of green vegetables.

6 oz (175g) continental lentils
1 large onion
2 tablespoonsful vegetable oil
2 eggs, hard-boiled
2 oz (50g) grated cheese
1 tablespoonful chopped parsley
2 teaspoonsful powdered mace, or to taste
2 oz (50g) wholemeal breadcrumbs
1 egg yolk
Sea-salt
Freshly-ground black pepper
Wholemeal flour
Vegetable oil for frying
Parsley sauce (see p.30) or tomato sauce (see p.31)

Cook lentils and drain. Peel onion and chop finely. Heat oil in medium-sized saucepan, add chopped onion, stir well, cover and cook gently for 15 minutes. Remove from heat. Chop hard-boiled eggs and add to the onions, together with remaining ingredients and cooked lentils. Mix well and season with salt and pepper.

When quite cold, shape into eight cutlets about $\frac{1}{2}$ inch (1cm) thick, coat with wholemeal flour and fry in shallow oil until well browned, turning carefully to brown second side (two or three minutes each side). Drain well on kitchen paper and serve with parsley or tomato sauce.

Serves 4.

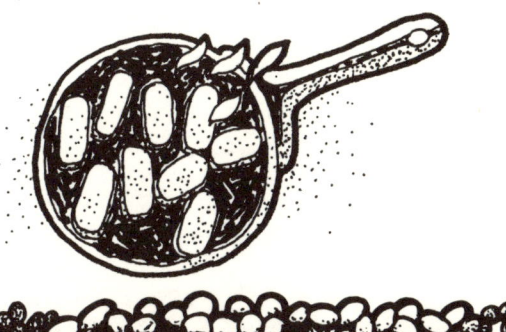

# Red Bean Pancakes with Soured Cream

Well worth making from scratch, but if you have leftover pancakes and beans in the freezer you can make a delicious lunch with minimum effort.

**8 oz (225g) fried red kidney beans (see p.86)**
**8 pancakes (see p.40)**
**1 carton soured cream**

Prepare the fried beans, mash down well with a fork and keep hot. Make the pancakes, or reheat ready-cooked pancakes over a pan of hot water. Fill pancakes with the bean mixture, roll up and arrange in a shallow ovenproof dish. Spoon the soured cream over the pancakes and place in a moderate oven for a few minutes to warm the cream.
    Serves 2.

## Black Bean Pancake Layer

Black beans are usual for this dish, but any cooked beans could be substituted. For a delicious blend of flavours, serve the pancake layer with plain, boiled, unpolished rice and guacamole sauce (see p.33).

**8 oz (225g) cooked black beans**
**2 tablespoonsful vegetable oil**
**1 small onion, peeled and chopped**
**2 teaspoonsful chopped parsley**
**1 teaspoonful chopped coriander** *or*
**1 teaspoonful coriander seeds, crushed**
**½ teaspoonful sea-salt, or to taste**
**Vegetable stock (see p.28)**
**8 pancakes (see p.40)**
**½ pt (275ml) chilli tomato sauce (see p.32)**

If using pancakes from the fridge or freezer, make sure that they are allowed to return to room temperature before use. Put the beans through a vegetable mill. Fry them briskly for a few minutes in the oil, then add the onion, parsley, coriander and salt. Continue frying for three to four minutes, stirring well. Add about half a teacupful of stock and simmer until the mixture becomes a thick *purée*.

Layer the pancakes in a baking dish, topping each one with bean *purée* and a tablespoonful of chilli tomato sauce. Finish with remaining sauce, cover with foil and place in a moderate oven, 350°F/180°C (Gas Mark 4) for 15-20 minutes or until heated through. Cut in wedges to serve.

Serves 3-4.

# Baked Stuffed Onions

A good winter supper dish. Cook jacket potatoes in the oven at the same time as the onions, and serve with green vegetables.

**4 large onions**
**1 large clove garlic**
**Vegetable oil**
**4 tablespoonsful** *purée* **of cooked beans, such as field beans, broad, red kidney or black beans (see p.14)**
**2 oz (50g) wholemeal breadcrumbs**
**1 tablespoonful ground, toasted soya beans (see p.21)**
**4 tablespoonsful finely chopped celery**
**2 teaspoonsful finely chopped parsley**
**½ teaspoonful dried thyme or marjoram**
**Sea-salt**
**Freshly-ground black pepper**
**Butter**
**2 teaspoonsful ground toasted soya beans, optional (see p.21)**

Peel onions and cut a thin slice off the base to make them stand level. Cut a slice from the top of each onion and carefully remove most of the centre. Use a pointed spoon such as a grapefruit spoon, leaving about three onion layers intact, and reserve the flesh.

Blanch the hollowed out onions in boiling water for about five minutes and drain carefully. Chop the reserved onion, peel and chop the garlic. Fry together in a little vegetable oil until beginning to soften.

Drain well and mix with the *purée* of beans, the breadcrumbs, ground soya beans, chopped parsley and celery. Season with thyme or marjoram, salt and pepper. Pack into the hollowed out onions, stand them in a small ovenproof dish and top each with a knob of butter. Cover and bake at 350°F/180°C (Gas Mark 4) for about 45 minutes. To brown the tops, the cooked onions may be sprinkled with ground soya beans, topped with a little more butter and finished under the grill.

Serves 4.

# Eggs Foo Yung

Serve hot with rice and sweet sour sauce (see p.33), or let the pancakes get cold and use them as sandwich fillings or in crusty rolls.

**4 oz (100g) bean sprouts**
**1 small onion**
**2 oz (50g) mushrooms**
**Vegetable oil**
**½ medium green pepper**
**6 eggs**
**2 teaspoonsful soya sauce, or to taste**
**Sea-salt**

Rinse bean sprouts, drain well and reserve. Peel and chop onion. Slice mushrooms. Cook onion gently in a little vegetable oil until beginning to soften. Add sliced mushrooms and cook for a few minutes longer. De-seed and chop the green pepper. Beat the eggs in a large basin until yolks and whites are just mixed. Season with soya sauce. Add drained bean sprouts, onion and mushroom mixture and a little salt, remembering that the soya sauce is already salty.

Wipe a large frying pan lightly with vegetable oil and cook the egg mixture in spoonfuls to make small pancakes, two or three at a time, turning to cook second side. Transfer to a serving dish and keep hot until all the mixture is used up.

Serves 2-3.

# 6
# SWEET DISHES

If you are afraid of the family thinking you eccentric, do not tell them you are putting beans in the cakes and puddings. Try Walnut Cookies or Cinnamon Creams and simply keep them guessing! There is no reason, after all, why some of the day's protein should not go into the pudding, and no reason why we should not use pulses in sweet dishes as they do in other countries.

# Cinnamon Creams

A delicious dessert reminiscent of chestnut *purée* – and a lot cheaper.

**1 lb (450g) cooked red kidney beans**
**1 pt (575ml) milk**
**4 oz (100g) light, soft, brown sugar**
**1 teaspoonful ground cinnamon**
**Double cream**
**Extra cinnamon to garnish**

Drain beans well, mix with the milk and reduce to a *purée* in the liquidizer. Rub through a sieve into a strong saucepan. Stir in sugar and cinnamon. Bring slowly to the boil over moderate heat, stirring well with a wooden spoon. Cook for four to five minutes, stirring constantly.

Now set the pan on a wire or asbestos mat over a low flame and cook for about 45 minutes, stirring occasionally, until mixture thickens. Cool and spoon into small china *soufflé* dishes. Serve cold but not chilled. Just before serving, top with a spoonful of unwhipped cream and a pinch of cinnamon.

Makes 6.

# Coconut Tart with Chocolate Sauce

May be prepared well ahead – just heat sauce gently before serving.

**Sweet shortcrust pastry made with 8 oz (225g) flour
(see p.35)
4 oz (100g) ground toasted chick peas (see p.20)
2 large eggs
6 tablespoonsful top milk or single cream
2 oz (50g) light, soft, brown sugar
1 teaspoonful grated orange peel
1 tablespoonful desiccated coconut
½ teaspoonful each ground nutmeg, cinnamon and
allspice
½ teaspoonful ground ginger
Pinch sea-salt**

*For the Sauce*
**2 tablespoonsful cocoa powder
5 tablespoonsful water
1 teaspoonful cornflour
2 tablespoonsful light, soft, brown sugar
½ oz (15g) butter**

Roll out pastry and line an 8-inch (20cm) pie plate. Chill while making filling. Put the ground chick peas in a pan with just under ½ pt (275ml) water and cook gently, stirring well, for about five minutes or until they form a thick paste, adding a little more water if necessary. Turn into a mixing bowl to cool. Beat the eggs and mix into the chick peas with the top milk, sugar, peel, coconut, spices and salt.

Spoon mixture into the pastry case and bake at 425°F/220°C (Gas Mark 7) for ten minutes, then reduce heat to 325°F/170°C (Gas Mark 3) for 20-30 minutes or until filling is set.

To make the sauce, cook the cocoa powder in the water for a few minutes, stirring to dissolve lumps. Mix cornflour with a little water and add to the pan with the sugar. Cook, stirring, until smooth and thick. Finally beat in the butter. Serve the tart cold with a little hot sauce spooned over each helping.

Serves 4-6.

## Spice and Nut Pudding

Any type of cooked beans may be used, so long as they are well drained to give a 'mealy' texture. The pudding may be cooked in one large basin if you prefer, in which case allow about two hours to cook.

**1 oz (25g) ground toasted soya beans (see p.21)**
**1 oz (25g) shelled walnuts, milled or finely chopped**
**2 oz (50g) wholemeal breadcrumbs**
**2 oz (50g) wholemeal flour**
**3 teaspoonsful baking powder**
**Pinch sea-salt**
**2 oz (50g) cooked beans**
**1 teaspoonful grated orange rind**
**½ teaspoonful ground ginger**
**½ teaspoonful ground cinnamon**
**4 oz (100g) margarine**
**4 oz (100g) light, soft, brown sugar**
**2 eggs**
**2 tablespoonsful honey**
**2-3 tablespoonsful Cereal Mix No.2 (see p.125)**
**Melted honey**

Put the ground soya beans in a large bowl with the milled nuts, breadcrumbs, flour, baking powder and salt. Make sure that the cooked beans are completely drained. Mill them or mash thoroughly and add to the bowl with the orange rind and spices.

Cream the margarine and sugar in a separate bowl. Beat the eggs in gradually with a little of the bean and flour mixture. Fold in the rest of the dry ingredients and mix together lightly. Butter four individual pudding moulds and put a little honey in the bottom of each. Divide pudding mixture between them. They should not be more than two-thirds full.

Cover tightly and steam for 30-40 minutes. Turn out and sprinkle with cereal mix. Serve with warmed honey.
Serves 4-6.

# Chocolate Cake

Adzuki beans are a favourite for sweet dishes, but the larger red kidney beans may be used instead. Sieving dry, cooked beans is rather laborious, and if they are well milled the skins are not obtrusive.

**6 oz (175g) cooked adzuki beans**
**4 oz (100g) margarine**
**4 oz (100g) light, soft, brown sugar**
**4 oz (100g) 81 per cent self-raising flour**
**2 teaspoonsful baking powder**
**1 oz (25g) cocoa powder**
**1 teaspoonful decaffeinated, instant coffee powder**
**Pinch sea-salt**
**2 eggs**

*For the Filling*
**4 oz (100g) cream cheese**
**2 oz (50g) light, soft, brown sugar**
**4 teaspoonsful cocoa powder**
**2 teaspoonsful decaffeinated, instant coffee powder**
**Desiccated or shredded coconut**

Make sure beans are soft and well drained. Put them twice through a vegetable mill, or mash and rub through a coarse-sieve to remove the skins. Cream margarine with sugar until light and fluffy.

In a separate bowl mix flour, baking powder, salt, coffee and cocoa. Beat eggs into creamed mixture, adding a little flour mix to prevent curdling. Gradually mix in remaining flour mix with the beans. Spoon into a greased and floured 9-inch (23cm) shallow cake tin and smooth top lightly. Bake at 350°F/180°C (Gas Mark 4) until risen and firm – about 25 minutes. Cool the cake in the tin for a few minutes, then turn out onto a wire rack.

To make the filling, beat cream cheese to soften, preferably with an electric mixer. Add sugar, cocoa and coffee powder and beat until smooth. When the cake is cold, split and spread with half the filling. Spread remainder over the top and sprinkle with coconut.

# Sandringham Tarts

Always a favourite, this recipe has extra flavour and goodness with added soya beans.

*For the Pastry*
**6 oz (175g) 81 per cent self-raising flour**
**2 oz (50g) ground toasted soya beans (see p.21)**
**2 oz (50g) margarine**
**2 oz (50g) white vegetable fat**
**4 tablespoonful milk**
**2 teaspoonful light, soft, brown sugar**
**Pinch sea-salt**

*For the Filling*
**4 oz (100g) margarine**
**4 oz (100g) light, soft, brown sugar**
**3 oz (75g) ground, toasted soya beans**
**3 oz (75g) ground rice**
**1 large egg**
**Vanilla flavouring (optional)**
**Tart-flavoured jam or jelly**

Make the pastry in the same way as sweet shortcrust (see p.35), mixing together the flour and toasted soya beans, and leave in a cool place while making the filling. Cream margarine and sugar. Add ground soya beans and rice with the egg and vanilla flavouring. Mix well.

Roll out pastry and cut into circles with a 3-inch (8cm) cutter. Line shallow patty tins. Put a little jam in each case, top with filling and smooth lightly with a fork. Bake at 400°F/200°C (Gas Mark 6) for ten minutes, then lower heat to 350°F/180°C (Gas Mark 4) for a further five to ten minutes or until filling is set. Cool on wire trays.
Makes about 20.

# Walnut Cookies

These are top of the 'fast disappearing' list among family cakes and bakes.

**3 oz (75g) butter**
**3 oz (75g) light, soft, brown sugar**
**2 oz (50g) 81 per cent plain flour**
**1 teaspoonful baking powder**
**Pinch sea-salt**
**1 oz (25g) Cereal Mix No.2 (see p.125)**
**1 oz (25g) ground, toasted soya beans**
**1 egg**
**2 oz (50g) demerara sugar**
**2 oz (50g) walnuts, coarsely chopped**

Cream butter and sugar. Mix flour, baking powder, sea-salt, cereal mix and ground soya beans. Separate the egg. Beat the yolk into the creamed mixture, adding dry ingredients gradually, to make a firm dough. Knead lightly until smooth, roll out about $\frac{1}{4}$-inch ($\frac{1}{2}$cm) thick and cut into $1\frac{1}{2}$-inch (4cm) circles with a pastry cutter. Brush with egg white and sprinkle with sugar. Press a few pieces of chopped walnut lightly into each biscuit.

Bake at 375°F/190°C (Gas Mark 5) on ungreased baking sheets for about twelve minutes or until golden. Allow to cool for two to three minutes, then remove carefully to a wire tray.

Makes about 20.

# Waffles

Waffles are always popular for family breakfasts, or if you precede them with a good mixed salad they make the basis of a light lunch. Serve with butter and honey, jam or cream cheese, or use one of the bean-based toppings on p.124. Use wholemeal flour if you prefer – the waffles will be just as tasty but not so light. If cereal mix is not available, make up the amount with more ground beans and flour.

**1 oz (25g) margarine**
**2 eggs**
**5 oz (150g) 81 per cent plain flour**
**1 oz (25g) ground, toasted soya beans (see p.21)**
**4 teaspoonsful baking powder**
**½ teaspoonful sea-salt**
**1 oz (25g) Cereal Mix No.2 (see p.125)**
**1 oz (25g) light, soft, brown sugar**
**⅓ pt (200ml) milk**

Melt the margarine and allow it to cool. Separate the eggs. Mix the flour, ground soya beans, baking powder and salt in a large bowl. Mix to a thick batter with the egg yolks, melted margarine and milk. Stir in the cereal mix and sugar. Whisk the egg whites stiffly and fold in. Cook on a well-greased waffle iron, using two to three tablespoonsful of batter for each waffle. Serve at once.

Makes about 8 circular waffles.

## Banana Bean Pancakes

An unlikely combination at first sight; this is a tasty recipe from Mexico where they have no inhibitions about mixing beans with almost any ingredient. A good sweet snack.

**3 very ripe bananas**
**3 oz (75g) wholemeal flour**
**1½ oz (45g) butter, melted and cooled**
**6 oz (175g) cooked red kidney beans**
**Sea-salt**
**Vegetable oil**
**Soft, brown sugar**
**Soured cream or natural yogurt**

Mash the bananas well, add the flour and butter and mix thoroughly. Heat a little oil in a frying pan. Spoon the banana mixture into the pan, one tablespoonful at a time, to make small pancakes, spreading and shaping the mixture with a fork. Fry over medium heat for five to six minutes, turning to brown second side. Transfer to heated dish and keep hot.

When all the pancakes are ready, fry the beans, mashing down with a wooden spoon and salting lightly. Top each pancake with a spoonful of beans, sprinkle with brown sugar and serve with soured cream or natural yogurt.

Serves 3-4.

# Dessert Topping

Make up this topping with any left over unsalted *purée* of cooked beans and keep in the fridge to use with desserts.

½ oz (15g) butter
**4 tablespoonsful bean *purée*, sieved (see p.14)**
**2 tablespoonsful honey**

Melt the butter in a small saucepan over low heat. Add bean *purée* and honey and mix well together. Use warm as a topping for pancakes, waffles, yogurt, ice-cream, etc.

*Flavourings*
*Coffee-orange.* Dissolve 2 teaspoonsful decaffeinated instant coffee in 3 tablespoonsful hot water and add to the sauce with 2 teaspoonsful finely grated orange rind.

*Mocha-orange.* As above, but with the addition of 2 teaspoonsful cocoa powder mixed to a paste with a little water. This gives a strongly flavoured sauce.

*Lemon.* Add 2 tablespoonsful lemon juice to basic topping.

*Lemon and banana.* Add 2 tablespoonsful lemon juice and 1 small, very ripe banana, well mashed.

*Coconut-orange.* Add 2 tablespoonsful desiccated coconut and 2 teaspoonsful finely grated orange rind to basic topping.

# Crunchy Breakfast

Use with milk and fresh or dried fruit, about two parts
Mix No.1 combined with one part Mix No.2.

*Mix No.1*
**2 oz (50g) toasted ground soya beans, finely ground
(see p.21)
1 oz (25g) unprocessed bran
1 oz (25g) rolled oats
2 oz (50g) milled walnuts or hazel nuts
2 oz (50g) light, soft, brown sugar
Pinch sea-salt**

Mix all ingredients well together and store in a screw
topped jar.

*Mix No.2*
**2 oz (50g) unsalted butter
2 oz (50g) toasted ground soya beans, finely ground
2 oz (50g) rolled oats
2 oz (50g) light, soft, brown sugar**

Melt the butter, cool slightly and add the ground soya
beans and rolled oats. Mix well and stir in the sugar.
Spread the mixture on the grill pan and toast under a
moderate grill for 10-15 minutes, stirring occasionally to
prevent burning. When well browned, allow the cereal
mix to get completely cold, then turn into a screw-topped
jar. Mix No.2 is best used within a few days, or it loses
crunchiness.

# INDEX